"Focusing more on the connections and less on the dichotomies between evangelical and liturgical churches, this illuminating book by Melanie Ross provides a timely and theologically profound description of evangelical worship. . . . Offers a groundbreaking, fascinating, and balanced understanding of the relationship between evangelicalism and contemporary liturgical Christianity. . . . Brilliant and refreshing."

— NATHAN D. MITCHELL
University of Notre Dame

"With biblical studies, theology, liturgical studies, and field research on her palette, Melanie Ross paints a nuanced, insightful picture of worship practices in our day. A tremendous resource for those engaged in ministry for whom worship practices and ecumenical relations are important, this is also a vital book for those who study the contemporary church in North America, offering new categories and definitions for their research."

— TODD E. JOHNSON
Fuller Theological Seminary

"This book is a passionate, heartfelt cry for embracing commonalities among all Christian churches while not ignoring the differences that may exist between liturgical and evangelical traditions. Ross calls for us to seek 'local middle ground' in order to overcome the false liturgical/evangelical dichotomy. Her call should resonate with all worshipping communities."

— JAMES R. HART
*Robert E. Webber Institute
for Worship Studies*

The CALVIN INSTITUTE OF CHRISTIAN WORSHIP LITURGICAL STUDIES Series, edited by John D. Witvliet, is designed to promote reflection on the history, theology, and practice of Christian worship and to stimulate worship renewal in Christian congregations. Contributions include writings by pastoral worship leaders from a wide range of communities and scholars from a wide range of disciplines. The ultimate goal of these contributions is to nurture worship practices that are spiritually vital and theologically rooted.

PUBLISHED

The Pastor as Minor Poet: Texts and Subtexts in the Ministerial Life
 M. Craig Barnes

Arts Ministry: Nurturing the Creative Life of God's People
 Michael J. Bauer

Touching the Altar: The Old Testament and Christian Worship
 Carol M. Bechtel, Editor

Resonant Witness: Conversations between Music and Theology
 Jeremy S. Begbie and Steven R. Guthrie, Editors

God against Religion: Rethinking Christian Theology through Worship
 Matthew Myer Boulton

From Memory to Imagination: Reforming the Church's Music
 C. Randall Bradley

By the Vision of Another World: Worship in American History
 James D. Bratt, Editor

Inclusive yet Discerning: Navigating Worship Artfully
 Frank Burch Brown

What Language Shall I Borrow? The Bible and Christian Worship
 Ronald P. Byars

A Primer on Christian Worship: Where We've Been, Where We Are, Where We Can Go
 William A. Dyrness

Christian Worship Worldwide: Expanding Horizons, Deepening Practices
 Charles E. Farhadian, Editor

Evangelical versus Liturgical?

Defying a Dichotomy

Melanie C. Ross

WILLIAM B. EERDMANS PUBLISHING COMPANY
GRAND RAPIDS, MICHIGAN / CAMBRIDGE, U.K.

Published 2014 by

Wm. B. Eerdmans Publishing Co.

2140 Oak Industrial Drive N.E., Grand Rapids, Michigan 49505 /

P.O. Box 163, Cambridge CB3 9PU U.K.

www.eerdmans.com

Printed in the United States of America

20 19 18 17 16 15 14   7 6 5 4 3 2 1

Library of Congress Cataloging-in-Publication Data

Ross, Melanie C.

Evangelical versus liturgical?: defying a dichotomy / Melanie C. Ross.

    pages   cm. — (Calvin Institute of Christian Worship liturgical studies series)

    Includes bibliographical references.

    ISBN 978-0-8028-6991-3 (pbk.: alk. paper)

    1. Liturgics — Case studies. 2. Evangelicalism. 3. Reformed Church —

    Doctrines.   I. Title.

BV178.R66   2014

264 — dc23

2014008409

For my parents,

   Bill and Janet,

      my first and best teachers of worship

Contents

Foreword

This book, though presenting its research calmly and moving carefully to thoughtful conclusions, has been written by an author with a mission. At first glance, *Evangelical versus Liturgical? Defying a Dichotomy* would seem to be on a fool's errand, for it reflects commitments to both the theoretical liturgical studies that have flourished in Roman Catholic and mainline Protestant circles as well as the worshipping lives of Protestant evangelicals for whom "liturgy" can sometimes sound like a dirty word. Yet by bringing together her mastery of standard authorities in the study of Christian liturgy and her own familiarity with evangelical traditions, Melanie Ross shows that, far from a fool's errand, this task can lead to edifying illumination.

The result of her pioneering effort is a challenge to scholars of liturgy to recognize that "free churches," which may be inert to traditional or formal liturgical studies, nonetheless can possess responsible (if unselfconscious) liturgical traditions. Along the way it shows that these churches have often developed insights about worship that formally trained liturgical scholars need to appreciate, and that these churches deserve a place at the table in liturgical study more generally.

But the book also aims a challenge at evangelicals by showing that formal liturgical studies pose no threat to the free churches, that the informal liturgies of evangelical churches may contain unrecognized problems, and that free churches would benefit from more liturgical self-consciousness.

Professor Ross has explored aspects of these themes in technical articles written primarily for scholars. With this book she shows that ordinary

Christians who are concerned about their own worship practices, along with scholars, can benefit by "defying a dichotomy."

The book's more theoretical discussions survey the very diverse landscape of American evangelicalism in order to argue that a "left of the right" (that is, liturgically aware evangelicals) and a "right of the left" (liturgical scholars beginning to take notice of evangelicals) have already begun to benefit from each other. This conclusion is well supported through careful engagement with important biblical scholars and theologians like Miroslav Volf and Kevin Vanhoozer, even as it sets out theoretical foundations for expanding those connections.

Readers who are not themselves liturgical scholars will, however, probably respond as I did in reading an earlier version of this volume. For me, the highlights were the empathetic descriptions of worship practices at a large Evangelical Free Church in Pennsylvania near Messiah College and an urban spin-off congregation of the Elmbrook ministries in Milwaukee. These chapters are particularly telling in showing how pastors and worship leaders at the two churches have worked self-consciously to enliven worship, relate it to the churches' broader goals, and inspire congregations to service — yet all without engaging the formal discourse of modern liturgical studies. It is particularly intriguing to read how the Milwaukee congregation has maintained a consistent evangelical theology while engaging in all manner of constructive community projects that liturgical scholars regularly suggest should flow from the best of liturgical renewal. In other words, this congregation is not engaged in that renewal, but it nonetheless sustains active medical service in the community, a wide welcome for immigrants, flourishing interracialism, and many other social-service projects — and all while proclaiming orthodox theological doctrines and making up its worship practices as it goes along.

With careful attention to current liturgical studies, serious understanding of important biblical and theological insights, and these truly outstanding reports from the field, the book should be of great interest to both welltrained liturgists and a considerable general audience. It strengthens the theology of worship but also shows how at least some active evangelical congregations have developed responsible norms for worship. It is a great asset as well that *Evangelical versus Liturgical?* is written with clear, graceful prose blissfully free of insider jargon.

As a whole, this book is enhanced by Professor Ross's broad reading in contemporary theology, both evangelical and other; it is marked by a solid grasp of American religious history; it reflects thorough knowledge of evangelical, mainline Protestant, and Roman Catholic liturgies; and it is particularly alert to how those liturgical practices have changed over time. Most importantly, it is a strategically important attempt to bridge the gaps that continue to divide the American Christian landscape between self-conscious liturgical scholars and dedicated evangelicals. The payoff from Melanie Ross's close attention to the day-to-day worshipping lives of ordinary American believers, her unusual measure of theological sophistication, and her deep liturgical learning is a feast for heart and mind in equal measure.

Mark A. Noll
University of Notre Dame

Acknowledgments

Many people have helped shepherd this project along its way, and it is a joy to publicly thank them for their extraordinary help. I am grateful to the William B. Eerdmans Publishing Company, Jon Pott, Mary Hietbrink, Michael Thomson, and John Witvliet, director of the Calvin Institute of Christian Worship. Warm thanks are also due to Kaudie McClean for her careful editorial work, and to my graduate assistant, Drew Konow, for his diligence.

This book began as a doctoral dissertation at the University of Notre Dame, and I am indebted to Nathan Mitchell, Maxwell Johnson, and Mark Noll for their generous encouragement and guidance of that project. I also wish to thank friends Rhodora Beaton, Kimberly Belcher, Katharine Harmon, Candace McLean, and Chris Brinks Rae, who read drafts, offered suggestions, and kept me laughing during the long slog that is dissertation-writing.

My friends in the Ministry and Missions Department at Huntington University — Karen Jones, Tom Bergler, Luke Fetters, and RuthAnn Price — have been important conversation partners throughout the project. If their students represent the next generation of evangelicalism, the future is very bright indeed.

The students, faculty, and staff of Yale Divinity School and Institute of Sacred Music defy theological dichotomies every day; it is a joy and a privilege to teach and work in such an environment. I am especially indebted to Greg Sterling, Dean of Yale Divinity School, and to Martin Jean, Director of the Yale Institute of Sacred Music. Thanks are also due to colleagues Teresa Berger and Bryan Spinks, who remain steadfast in their support and advice.

Were it not for Siobhán Garrigan, I would not be doing this work at all. Over the last ten years, her wisdom and friendship have shaped this book, and its author, more deeply than words can say.

Martha Moore-Keish has supplied theological acumen and pastoral care in equal parts throughout the book-writing journey. I give thanks to her, and to Chris, Miriam, and Fiona, for their generous hospitality and for many joyous conversations around the dinner table.

I am grateful to Todd Johnson, Gordon Lathrop, Don Saliers, and the members of the liturgical theology study group at the North American Academy of Liturgy for reading and commenting on several sections of the book.

An army of people has helped shape this book in less direct but equally significant ways. Heartfelt thanks go to Geoff and Callista Isabelle; Lawrie Merz and John McGuire; Evie Telfer; Neil, Joanie, and my "Rostrander" siblings Caleb and Olivia; Doug and Heidi Curry; Paul and Cathy Morgan; Geoff and Vicki Twigg; Paul, Sally, and John Zink; Jim and Tracey Strohecker; and Kathy Buck and her late husband, Stan. Potpie the cat offered hours of delightful distraction, and grudgingly tolerated the computer that so often usurped his rightful place on my lap.

Very special thanks are due to the congregations of West Shore Evangelical Free Church and Eastbrook Church. In 2009-2010, both congregations showered me with hospitality, answered my questions cheerfully, invited me into family homes, welcomed me into worship services, choir rehearsals, and prayer meetings, and trusted me with their stories. If there is anything praiseworthy in the pages that follow, it comes as a direct result of time spent with these churches. (The faults that remain are entirely my own.) Both congregations have experienced demographic and leadership shifts between the time of my research and the book's publication, and I watch with excitement to see how God will be at work in the next chapters of their stories.

I give thanks for two important pastors in my life: Johnny Miller, who has been a spiritual father and mentor, and John Frye, who continues to teach me to worship in spirit and in truth.

Finally, this book could not have been written without the prayers of my grandparents and the pies and phone calls of my sister Heather. But most of all, I wish to thank my parents, Bill and Janet Ross. With no thought of recognition, they have quietly poured their lives into supporting their children, their extended families, and their church. It is with respect, deep gratitude, and all my love that I dedicate the book to them.

MCR
New Haven, Connecticut

The Formation of a Dichotomy

Often the truth is in the complex middle, not the oversimplified extremes.

Deborah Tannen, *The Argument Culture*

Since the mid-nineteenth century, scientists and mathematicians have suggested that the world organizes itself around bell-shaped averages. Whether measuring the length of people's middle fingers, the average of students' test scores, or the price of certain goods over time, the organizational majority tends to be centrally located, with minority exceptions pushed to the edges. Recently, however, the bell shape has undergone an inversion. Scholars are giving attention to the collapse of middles and the rise of a phenomenon that Daniel Pink has named the "well curve."[1]

The distribution of the well curve is low in the center and high on the sides, and anecdotal evidence for it abounds in daily life. Electronics manufacturers produce screens small enough for cell phones or large enough for home theaters, rendering standard-size screens obsolete. Walmart and specialty boutiques thrive; mid-size department stores struggle. In education, the percentage of students scoring in the highest and the lowest test percentiles has increased; the number of those scoring in the middle has

1. See Daniel H. Pink, "The Shape of Things to Come," *Wired*, May 2003, at http://www .wired.com/wired/archive/11.05/start.html?pg=2.

dropped. Even the notion of "middle class" is quickly becoming obsolete: the Federal Reserve reports the fastest rates of growth at the top and the bottom of the economic spectrum.

Of course, not everything we can measure conforms to this new shape. Pink points out that the fastest-growing political affiliation is Independent, and that diversity and interracial marriage are rendering the old bimodal and trimodal racial categories irrelevant. Nevertheless, he concludes, "almost everywhere we look closely we find ourselves staring down a distributional well. Our tastes and choices are shifting away from the middle and toward the extremes."[2]

The concept of the well curve helps make sense of a persistent pattern in liturgical studies — one that pits evangelical churches against the liturgical renewal movement and allows for little ground in between. Consider the following examples. Richard Giles, a contributor to the Liturgical Press blog, Pray Tell, recounts receiving a flyer in the mail advertising a new, nondenominational church in a nearby town — one that boasts a bookstore, a coffee shop, state-of-the-art worship facilities, and seating for 2,000 people. Although he has never set foot inside the church personally, Giles used the flyer as a caution: "We must accept that for most worshippers in nondenominational evangelicalism, 'liturgy' is a dirty word, or at least an incomprehensible one. . . . They regard the sacred liturgy, set texts, and lectionaries of the Church with suspicion and understand liturgy as only a quenching of the Spirit and the 'heaping up of empty phrases' warned against by Our Lord. The incomparable treasures of our tradition mean nothing to them," he concludes.[3] Author Graham Hughes suggests a reason for this aversion: "An interest in 'liturgy' as a matter for historical inquiry, morphological analysis, or theological inspection is seen precisely as characteristic of the kinds of Christianity from which [evangelicals] wish to distinguish themselves."[4]

Evangelicals are indeed more prone to speak of "worship" than they are of "liturgy" or "rite" — a posture that baffles and frustrates their Catholic and Orthodox colleagues. "An aliturgical Christian church is as much

2. Pink, "The Shape of Things to Come."

3. See Richard Giles, "The Challenge of Non-Liturgical Churches," at http://www.praytell-blog.com/index.php/2010/02/04/the-challenge-of-non-liturgical-churches/.

4. Graham Hughes, *Worship as Meaning: A Liturgical Theology for Late Modernity* (Cambridge: Cambridge University Press, 2003), p. 234.

a contradiction in terms as a human society without language," Aidan Kavanagh protests.[5] David Fagerberg concurs: "A non-leitourgia assembly is oxymoronic to Christian tradition."[6] Furthermore, Gordon Lathrop charges evangelicals with replacing the ecumenical fourfold *ordo* (word, bath, table, and prayer) with a threefold *ordo* of their own making (warm-up, sermon, conversion). "Where are the scriptures in your meetings," Lathrop probes, "let alone baptism and the supper?"[7]

Perhaps Robert Webber summarizes the dichotomy best by distinguishing between "separatist" and "ecumenical" evangelicals. The former are persons, congregations, or denominations who "define themselves over against Catholic, Orthodox, and mainline Protestant denominations, do not participate in the National Council of Churches or the World Council of Churches, and are usually uninvolved with local ministerial groups."[8] The latter are those who campaign for "a return to weekly Eucharist, a recognition of real presence, [and] the restoration of the church year," along with "the use of ritual, gesture, bodily action, vestments, and other ceremonials."[9] Ecumenical evangelicals, Webber observes, are often repentant Separatists who have entered into mainline, Orthodox, Catholic, and Episcopal churches.

The polarities sketched above are excellent examples of the "well curve" phenomenon. All use the rhetoric of "us" versus "them." All posit only two evangelical approaches to liturgical reform: *either* a wholehearted embrace (convergence) *or* an outright rejection (separatism). The "middle" — evangelicals who respect and appreciate other Christian traditions that preach from lectionary texts, pray with fixed liturgies, and celebrate a weekly Eucharist but have chosen not to adopt these forms for their own worship — has collapsed.

5. Aidan Kavanagh, *On Liturgical Theology* (Yonkers, N.Y.: Pueblo Publishing Co., 1992), p. 120.

6. David W. Fagerberg, *Theologia Prima: What Is Liturgical Theology?*, 2nd ed. (Chicago: Hillenbrand Books, 2004), p. 112.

7. Gordon Lathrop, "New Pentecost or Joseph's Britches? Reflections on the History and Meaning of the Worship Ordo in the Megachurches," *Worship* 76, no. 6 (2001): 537.

8. Robert E. Webber, "The Impact of the Liturgical Movement on the Evangelical Church," *Reformed Liturgy and Music* 21, no. 2 (1987): 111.

9. Webber, "The Impact of the Liturgical Movement on the Evangelical Church," p. 113.

How This Book Came to Be

The notion of "middle" is important to me because I live with one foot in both evangelical and liturgical worlds. When I first entered the world of liturgical studies, I was confused by a lexicon of words I had never encountered in my nondenominational church: *anamnesis, epiclesis, homily, lectionary,* and *antiphon,* to cite but a few examples. Over a decade later, I continue to do a great deal of translation work when I talk to my family and church friends about my chosen academic discipline. I am sympathetic to honest critiques of my tradition: evangelicals should be engaged in deeper study of sacramental practices, ecumenical creeds, and the liturgical year. Resources abound for introducing these topics, and I use them regularly in my teaching.

At the same time, I keep in mind John Witvliet's caution:

> It is terribly tempting to teach worship with an undertone of guilt ("if you don't do it this way, be shamed"), fear ("worship practices out there are pretty bad, and getting worse"), or pride ("how fine indeed it is that we don't pray like those [fill in the blank] publicans").[10]

Witvliet stresses that "even in the bleakest days," the most fitting "gospel undertone" for discussions of worship is gratitude.[11] So, in addition to introducing my low-church evangelical students to the riches of Catholic, Orthodox, and mainline Protestant liturgical traditions, I want to help them see that they themselves have important gifts to bring to the ecumenical table.

However, this book was born out of the discovery that little translation work was being done in the opposite direction: it was — and continues to be — difficult to find academic literature that explains "low church" evangelical worship practices to those from more "high church" liturgical traditions. In 1989, liturgical historian James White noted that evangelicalism had been "almost totally ignored in liturgical scholarship, as if such an omnipresent American phenomenon did not deserve description, still less interpreta-

---

10. John D. Witvliet, "Teaching Worship as a Christian Practice," in *For Life Abundant: Practical Theology, Theological Education, and Christian Ministry,* ed. Dorothy C. Bass and Craig Dykstra (Grand Rapids: Wm. B. Eerdmans, 2008), p. 143.

11. Witvliet, "Teaching Worship as a Christian Practice," p. 144.

tion."[12] Fourteen years later, in 2003, liturgical theologian Graham Hughes reported little change in the scholarly landscape: "One faces an unmapped (possibly hazardous) territory in attempting to include evangelical Christianity in an account of liturgical theology. . . . This style of worship is simply bypassed in discussions of liturgical theology."[13] White and Hughes sound similar notes of caution to their mainline and Catholic colleagues. "We face a basic problem in ignoring the worship of most North American Christians," says White; and Hughes comments that "as a highly prominent way of making sense of 'God' in our times, [evangelicalism] belongs in an account of liturgical meaning production."[14]

White, Hughes, and a handful of other liturgical scholars have taken steps to address the lacuna, and I am appreciative of their pioneering work. But as an individual with deep academic and experiential knowledge of evangelicalism, I find their scholarship problematic on a number of levels. Too many historical accounts of evangelical worship fixate on the controversial innovations of Charles Finney and neglect the ecumenical vision of earlier evangelical leaders. Too many liturgical scholars use the words "fundamentalism" and "evangelicalism" interchangeably, despite the fact that historians like Mark Noll, George Marsden, and Joel Carpenter have spent thirty years nuancing the definitions of both terms. Too many descriptions of evangelical worship are written by mainline scholars on the basis of isolated visits or secondhand reports. Most of these accounts are now decades out of date and describe a "seeker-service" model whose influence has waned significantly among evangelicals.[15] There is pressing need for work that brings together the best of liturgical scholarship with the best scholarship on American evangelicalism and puts both in conversation with worship practices of contemporary congregations. I hope this book is one small step in that direction.

Purpose for book.

---

12. James F. White, *Protestant Worship: Traditions in Transition* (Louisville: Westminster John Knox Press, 1989), p. 171.

13. Hughes, *Worship as Meaning*, p. 234.

14. James F. White, "How Do We Know It Is Us?" in *Liturgy and the Moral Self: Humanity at Full Stretch before God*, ed. E. Anderson and B. Morrill (Collegeville, Minn.: Liturgical Press, 1998), pp. 57-58; Hughes, *Worship as Meaning*, p. 234.

15. See Chapter 4 for more details.

The Shape of This Book

In the chapters that follow, I draw on historical analyses of the evangelical movement, an ecumenical comparison of systematic theologies, and the worship life of two vibrant congregations to argue that the common ground that evangelical and liturgical churches share is no less important than the differences that divide them. My thesis is that the discipline of liturgical studies must be both more historical and more theological in its assessment of evangelical worship, which in turn will require a rethinking of the evangelical-liturgical relationship.

In Chapter One, I explain the difference between evangelical and liturgical churches as the clash of two *ordos*. Liturgical scholarship in the twentieth century was marked by the search for the *ordo* — the "shape" of the liturgy" that has united Christians throughout the ages. *Ordo* means more than a congregation's printed order of songs, Scripture readings, and responses. It is the animating principle of the liturgy, the "deep structure" that remains constant even as "surface structures" shift from one Sunday to the next. Broadly conceived, the *ordo* of the liturgy is rooted in four primary symbols: word, bath, table, and prayer. These symbols take on meaning in action; indeed, it is precisely their juxtaposition that makes for the Christian distinctiveness of the liturgical event. To speak of the ecumenical *ordo*, then, is to speak of a transcultural, transdenominational pattern that has endured in Christian worship from the second century to the present day.

However, many liturgical scholars worry that this ancient ecumenical pattern has been threatened by a pervasive, theologically inferior "frontier *ordo*" that first came to prominence in nineteenth-century American revivals. The trajectory of this frontier *ordo* can be traced from Charles Finney to Billy Graham to Bill Hybels and Willow Creek. Its threefold shape — preliminary songs that "soften up" an audience, a fervent sermon, and an altar call for new converts — effectively marginalizes the Lord's Supper. The audience's attention is drawn from the glory of the risen Christ to the magnetic personality of the speaker. Worship is simply the means to an evangelistic end, rather than an end in and of itself. But by focusing so narrowly on Finney's controversial innovations, liturgical scholars have lost sight of the evangelical movement's historical commitment to ecumenism. To this end, I introduce the bridge-building work of Finney's predecessor, George Whitefield, and argue for its significance in rethinking the evangelical-liturgical relationship today.

Chapter Three begins with an irony: the Bible — recognized by all Christians as the supreme authority of faith and life — is a sticking point in ecumenical conversation. In the last thirty years, increasing methodological diversity in biblical studies has led to decreasing consensus about the nature of Scripture's authority. Systematic theologians tend to paint evangelicals and fundamentalists with the same broad brush: their insistence on the propositional truth of Scripture betrays conceptual brittleness and naïveté. However, these charges misrepresent the evangelical movement as a whole and are a major stumbling block to the ecumenical dialogue for which this book calls. In the first half of the chapter, I suggest that evangelical, Roman Catholic, and mainline scholars are, in fact, united by a common concern: dispelling a popular "dropped from the sky" understanding of the Bible that comes dangerously close to textual deification. I support this claim by placing the work of evangelical theologians John Webster and Kevin Vanhoozer in conversation with the biblical-liturgical scholarship of Aidan Kavanagh, Louis Marie Chauvet, and Gordon Lathrop. I then proceed to compare the correctives of Webster and Vanhoozer to those offered by Kavanagh, Chauvet, and Lathrop. Whereas the liturgical scholars agree that the solution to fundamentalism is returning Scripture to its rightful liturgical context, evangelicals are unwilling to award tradition the same authority as Scripture. However, evangelicals make their own distinctive contribution by emphasizing the Trinitarian nature of revelation and taking seriously the diversity of biblical genres.

Chapter Four addresses a central question in evangelical-liturgical dialogue: Is the church centered on individuals, their processes of decision-making, and escaping the fleshly conditions of life (a gnostic ecclesiology), or is the church created by God-given concrete and communal means (a sacramental ecclesiology)? Following Gordon Lathrop, many liturgical scholars worry that the characteristics of the frontier *ordo* — Scripture verses that accent technique, an emphasis on the individual, no meal, and little sense of assembly — place evangelicals closer to the former position than the latter.

I contest the premise of this false dichotomy by facilitating a dialogue between Lathrop and systematic theologian Miroslav Volf with the intent of establishing a more nuanced evangelical ecclesiology. Most evangelicals

do not feel compelled to choose between personal faith and communal sacraments. They maintain a both/and position: although there is no church
without the sacraments, neither are there sacraments without the individual
confession of faith. I then build on the biblical scholarship of Raymond
Brown to argue that the roots of evangelical ecclesiology lie closer to the
Fourth Gospel than to early Gnostic heresies. Neither sacraments nor the
concept of church structure lies at the heart of the Johannine community's concept of itself: instead, liturgy and ecclesiology are subservient to the
person of Jesus and a personal relationship to him. The Johannine/Synoptic
relationship provides a promising new paradigm for understanding evangelicalism's relationship to liturgical Christianity today: the two traditions
are more symbiotic than contradictory.

Throughout the project, I advocate for a "hermeneutic of charity" over a
"hermeneutic of suspicion" in the study of evangelical worship. These terms,
which come from Richard Mouw's book *Consulting the Faithful: What Christian Intellectuals Can Learn from Popular Religion,* offer a helpful reference
point for ecumenical discussion.[16] Mouw argues that good scholarship will
always give the other at least some benefit of the doubt, especially when the
"other" is a fellow Christian. Evangelical scholar James K. A. Smith explains
the "hermeneutic of charity" this way: it is "the sense that, no matter how
much I might disagree and be frustrated by [evangelical] positions and interpretations, I know that above all my brothers and sisters want to be faithful
disciples of Jesus."[17]

Gordon Lathrop makes a conciliatory step in this direction when he
suggests that megachurches can teach liturgical churches many things: "the
awareness that numerous people today have no understanding at all [of] the
traditions and conventions of Christianity; the honesty that Christianity is
genuinely in a marketplace of cultural products; the courage to welcome
emotions into the assembly of the people of God; the openness to the strang-
er."[18] The problem with this list of attributes is that it is generic and practical,

16. Richard J. Mouw, *Consulting the Faithful: What Christian Intellectuals Can Learn from
Popular Religion* (Grand Rapids: Wm. B. Eerdmans, 1994), p. 13.
17. James K. A. Smith, *The Devil Reads Derrida — and Other Essays on the University, the
Church, Politics, and the Arts* (Grand Rapids: Wm. B. Eerdmans, 2009), pp. xv-xvi.
18. Lathrop, "New Pentecost or Joseph's Britches?," p. 536.

not doctrinal or doxological. Because nothing within it points to the distinctiveness of Christianity, it might easily describe *any* religious tradition.

Differences between evangelical and liturgical churches are real, and unresolved: they deserve to be named and engaged by scholars from across denominational traditions. These differences are not, however, dichotomous — a fact evidenced by the case studies of Chapters Two and Five. The congregations of Eastbrook Church in Milwaukee, Wisconsin, and West Shore Evangelical Free Church in Mechanicsburg, Pennsylvania, make substantive contributions to the ecumenical study of Christian worship. As I hope to show in the pages that follow, these churches — and countless others like them across the country — provide dynamic, living proof that the "well curve" between evangelical and liturgical churches is not nearly as great as many scholars have feared.

CHAPTER ONE

Pragmatism versus Ecumenism?
Rethinking Historical Origins

Pragmatic: a way based on practical rather than theoretical considerations

The solution, of course . . . is for evangelicals to take stock theologically of what constitutes biblical worship, the real purpose and ministry of the church, and genuine Christian piety. But that kind of stock-taking would undo evangelicalism. For it would send evangelicals off to the riches of the Reformed, Lutheran, and Anglican traditions where these matters have been defined and articulated and where worship is the logical extension of a congregation's confession of faith and lies at the heart of the church's mission.

D. G. Hart, "Why Evangelicals Think They Hate Liturgy"

We're not going directly back to the early church, or the patristic era, or to Luther and Calvin. That's impossible. The analogy that works for me is that Christian traditions are like tributaries, and evangelicalism tries to create waterways between them. But by incorporating liturgical elements into our tradition, we're not becoming theirs. Or, to switch analogies, it's like grafting traditional practices onto an evangelical tree that already has its identity. In so doing, we're becoming a more adult, mature, sophisticated version of what we already are: a from-below, pietist, pragmatist, revivalist, baptistic tradition.

Pastor Phil Thorne, West Shore Evangelical Free Church

"Evangelical" is a notoriously difficult word to define. When a liturgical scholar steps across disciplinary lines to ask systematic theologians, sociologists, and church historians to identify its essence, she is immediately confronted with a dizzying array of conflicting responses. Some have quipped that an evangelical is anyone who admires Billy Graham. Randall Balmer proposes a twofold definition: the centrality of conversion and a belief that the Bible is God's Word and therefore lies at the core of the Christian life.[1] The majority of evangelical scholars acknowledge that "no other definition comes close" to rivaling David Bebbington's "quadrangle" of biblicism, conversionism, crucicentrism, and activism as the essence of evangelicalism.[2]

Interestingly, the most cohesive contemporary metaphors for evangelicalism — "mosaic," "kaleidoscope," "family resemblance," and "patchwork quilt" — are images that deliberately undermine the notion of center. Therefore, some scholars have taken refuge in an apophatic methodology, choosing to define evangelicalism by what it is not. For example, Roger Olson describes evangelicalism as an unstable compound held together by the twin enemies of liberal Protestantism and separatistic fundamentalism.[3] George Marsden quips that little holds evangelicalism together "other than common traditions, a central one of which is the denial of the authority of traditions."[4] Arguing that "evangelicalism" is too heterogeneous, theologically diverse, and institutionally pluriform a movement to fit comfortably under one label, critic Donald Dayton has called for "a moratorium on the use of the term [evangelical], in the hope that we would be forced to more appropriate and useful categories of analysis."[5]

Liturgical historian James White confronted this terminological di-

1. Randall Herbert Balmer and Lauren F. Winner, *Protestantism in America* (New York: Columbia University Press, 2002), p. 71.

2. Timothy Larsen, "Defining and Locating Evangelicalism," in *The Cambridge Companion to Evangelical Theology,* ed. Timothy Larsen and Daniel J. Treier (Cambridge and New York: Cambridge University Press, 2007), p. 1.

3. Roger E. Olson, "Response: The Reality of Evangelicalism: A Response to Michael S. Horton," *Christian Scholar's Review* 31 (2001): 161.

4. George Marsden, *Understanding Evangelicalism and Fundamentalism* (Grand Rapids: Wm. B. Eerdmans, 1991), p. 81.

5. Donald Dayton, "Some Doubts about the Usefulness of the Category 'Evangelical,'" in *The Variety of American Evangelicalism,* ed. Donald W. Dayton and Robert K. Johnston (Knoxville: University of Tennessee Press, 1991), p. 245.

lemma in his book *Protestant Worship: Traditions in Transition*. White reported a startling lacuna in liturgical studies: "The most prevalent worship
tradition in American Protestantism (and maybe in American Christianity)
lacks any recognized name" and "has been almost totally ignored in liturgical
scholarship."[6] As a corrective, White created a new liturgical category to describe North American evangelicalism. He named it the "Frontier tradition"
and defined its parameters: "Essentially, the frontier extends in time for a
century after the Revolution and in space from the Appalachians to the West
Coast. Kentucky, Tennessee, and western New York were the key areas in
shaping the Frontier tradition in worship."[7] Charles Finney (1792-1875), a
man White nominates as possibly "the most influential liturgical reformer
in American history,"[8] served as the representative spokesperson for the
new tradition.

The Pragmatism of Charles Finney

According to White, Charles Finney and his followers faced an unprecedented challenge: Protestant worship was still operating within the world
of Christendom when it reached the American frontier. In the European
tradition, Christianity was something one was born into. For example, the
Anglican Church didn't develop a rite for "Baptism of such as are of Riper
Years" until as late as 1662. Even for Methodism in England, there were few
adults to be baptized except for occasional Quaker converts. White stresses
that although several traditions practiced evangelistic preaching outside of
the church, none of them developed a whole system of worship that led
to baptism rather than leading *from* it.[9] In developing just such a system,
American churches were forced to contend with an unprecedented logistical
difficulty: How would they minister to a largely unchurched and uneducated
population scattered over enormous distances of thinly settled land?

An initial answer was found in the form of sacramental seasons, a prac-

6. James F. White, *Protestant Worship: Traditions in Transition* (Louisville: Westminster
John Knox Press, 1989), p. 171.

7. White, *Protestant Worship*, p. 172.

8. White, *Protestant Worship*, p. 176.

9. White, *Protestant Worship*, p. 171.

tice that originated in Scotland and was brought to the colonies in the seventeenth century. These seasons, which drew thousands of people from all over the region, were several-day-long festivals that consisted of preaching services leading to the celebration of the Eucharist. In time the Eucharistic service

> came to be dwarfed by the tent-preaching, the outdoor crowds of strangers which no one screened, the extensive campsites, the entertainments, and the spiritual seizures and displays which surrounded it. Indeed, the "preparation" went on for days after the communion service was over, that service no longer being the goal of the event. Many subsequent sacrament meetings on the frontier came to be marked by the same displays and the same growing marginalization of the sacrament itself.[10]

Sacramental seasons gatherings provided a massive attraction amid the loneliness and colorlessness of the American frontier experience: they were fun and, for many, emotionally fulfilling. When the Eucharistic portion dropped out of the services, the individual's decision became paramount. Communion was still practiced, "but, just as in the Middle Ages, now made very much less important than the new forms of the process of contrition and penance."[11]

The First Great Awakening (1725-1750) resulted in a restatement of Calvinism in which an individual became somewhat more responsible for working out his or her salvation. Theologians of the time asserted that "man had the natural ability to act rightly, but he was morally unable to do so unless God, through the Holy Spirit, transformed or infused his soul with grace."[12] However, the Second Great Awakening (1795-1835) saw a further, more dramatic breakdown of Calvinism. In contrast to Jonathan Edwards's renowned thesis on revival, "A Faithful Narrative of the Surprising Work of God" (1737), Finney's most famous revival sermon was "Sinners Bound to Change Their Own Hearts" (1836). The difference in titles clearly illustrates the theological tension between the two Awakenings.

10. Gordon W. Lathrop, "New Pentecost or Joseph's Britches? Reflections on the History and Meaning of the Worship Ordo in the Megachurches," *Worship* 72, no. 6 (1998): 528.

11. Lathrop, "New Pentecost or Joseph's Britches?," p. 529.

12. Charles Grandison Finney, *Lectures on Revivals of Religion* (Cambridge, Mass.: Belknap Press, 1960), p. xii.

In addition to a shift in theology, the period between the beginning of the First Awakening and the end of the Second saw a shift in methodology. In 1734 Jonathan Edwards described revival as "a marvelous work of God" and a "shower of divine blessing" that came to a parched land from the hand of God.[13] One hundred years later, Charles Finney asserted that the church should not sit back idly and wait for revival to mysteriously fall from the sky. Revival instead resulted from "the right use of appropriate means."[14] Finney united traditional revival means such as preaching, prayer, and repentance with what came to be known as the "new measures," which included door-to-door visitations, allowing women to testify in mixed gatherings, and protracted meetings that lasted several days. Arguably the most controversial new measure, however, was Finney's employment of "the anxious bench," a seat in which "the anxious may come and be addressed particularly and be made subjects of prayer."[15]

Strictly speaking, the anxious bench was not a "new" measure, although its history is difficult to document. Revivalists prior to Finney sometimes used Inquiry Meetings — meetings separate from the revival services in which interested persons could seek further advice about the their souls' welfare.[16] A similar practice was also employed at the famous revivals of 1801 in Cane Ridge, Kentucky, where as many as twenty-five thousand people gathered. A crowd so large was difficult to control, and the "indiscriminate distribution of the participants" resulted in charges of immorality that perhaps contained an element of truth.[17] One measure for controlling the mob was to collect the "mourners" (sinners) and seat them in the front of the crowd. Scholars are uncertain as to how conscious Finney was of his borrowing, but in 1820, Finney combined the ideology of the Inquiry Meetings and the practice of bringing mourners to the front of the congregation into the form known as the anxious bench.

13. Edwards, quoted by William G. McLoughlin in his introduction to Charles G. Finney, *Lectures on Revivals of Religion* (Cambridge, Mass.: Belknap Press, 1960), p. x.

14. Finney, *Lectures on Revivals of Religion*, p. 13.

15. Finney, *Lectures on Revivals of Religion*, p. 267.

16. Bill J. Leonard, "Getting Saved in America: Conversion Event in a Pluralistic Culture," *Review and Expositor* 82 (Winter 1995): 120.

17. See Thomas H. Olbricht, "The Invitation: A Historical Survey," in *Restoration Quarterly*, at http://www.restorationquarterly.org/Volume_005/rq005010olbricht.htm.

For Finney, the end justified the means. Methodology was not important so long as souls were being brought to Christ, and Finney could not understand why his new tactics drew such harsh criticism. In his final lecture, "Growth in Grace," Finney drew a parallel between an election campaign and a revival. In political spheres, the concern is not whether new or old measures are used, but rather if the candidate wins the election. Finney saw no reason for the spiritual realm to operate any differently.[18] In Finney's interpretation, Jesus himself was more concerned with results than with forms:

> When Jesus Christ was on earth . . . he had nothing to do with forms or measures. . . . The Jews accused him of disregarding their forms. His object was to preach and teach mankind the true religion. . . . No person can pretend to get a set of forms or particular directions as to measures out of [the Great Commission]. Their [the apostles'] goal was to make known the gospel in the *most effectual way.*[19]

Finney believed that the "most effectual way" of producing converts was through a threefold *ordo* still followed in many evangelical churches: (1) preliminary songs, readings, and dramas prepare the congregation to receive (2) the message of preaching, after which individuals are encouraged to (3) make a decision for Christ. Proponents of the new measures and the threefold *ordo* enthused that if God had chosen to operate in a certain way, they were in no position to find fault or condemn: if God has "owned it, impressed his seal upon it, and works through it mightily" as a means to salvation, who are we to criticize?[20] In short, Charles Finney saw a church that had retained its outward structures but lost its heart. In his eyes, the church of his day had fallen soundly asleep. New measures were necessary for a church that seemed to repeatedly "wake up, rub [its] eyes, bluster about and vociferate a little while, and then go off to sleep again."[21]

Finney's contemporaries vehemently protested the assertion that churches which relied on old measures and forms retained the form of religion while

18. Finney, *Lectures on Revivals of Religion*, p. 251.

19. Finney, quoted in Olbricht, "The Invitation: A Historical Survey," p. 251.

20. John Williamson Nevin, *The Anxious Bench; The Mystical Presence* (New York: Garland Publishing, 1987), p. 12.

21. Finney, *Lectures on Revivals of Religion*, p. 11.

losing its substance.[22] Most outspoken was John Nevin (1803-1886), a professor at the German Reformed Church Seminary, who decried Finney's new
measures in his 1843 work, *The Anxious Bench*. In Nevin's assessment, Finney
had exchanged the stability of old forms for the tyranny of the ever-changing
new, and his reliance on novelty was "the refuge of weakness."[23] Trusted measures such as creeds, catechisms, and ordinary pastoral ministrations *did* have
virtue, and if a minister had no power in a catechetical class, then he deceived
himself if he thought he would gain power through the use of the anxious
bench. Nevin argued, "If it be true that the old forms are dead and powerless in
a minister's hands, the fault is not in the forms, but in the minister himself; and
it is the very impotence of quackery to think of mending the case essentially by
the introduction of new forms."[24] One of Nevin's most important claims was
that the "inward must be the bearer of the outward,"[25] and the new measures
were quackery because they inverted this order. In the case of the anxious
bench, Nevin feared that sinners would rely on an intense outward experience
that was incapable of sustaining a deep inward transformation.

Today, Nevin's concerns have been taken up by liturgical scholars who
worry that the invisible, "born-again" experience of evangelicalism has come
to trump the significance of visible ecclesial structures. For example, when
evangelical theologian Donald Carson states that "from an evangelical perspective, it is not strictly *necessary* to list the sacraments/ordinances as one
of the defining marks of the church," critics hear a devaluation of the visible
church.[26] Accordingly, Simon Chan cautions evangelicals against a "docetic
ecclesiology where the 'real' church is perceived as spiritual, inward, and
invisible and has no correlation with the visible church."[27] D. G. Hart goes so
far as to argue that if evangelicals took theological stock of what constitutes
biblical worship, the real purpose and ministry of the church, and genuine

---

22. Finney, *Lectures on Revivals of Religion,* p. 269.

23. Nevin, *The Anxious Bench,* p. 23.

24. Nevin, *The Anxious Bench,* p. 22.

25. Nevin, *The Anxious Bench,* p. 20.

26. D. A. Carson, "Evangelicals, Ecumenism, and the Church," in *Evangelical Affirma-
tions,* ed. Kenneth S. Kantzer and Carl F. H. Henry (Grand Rapids: Academie Books, 1990),
p. 376.

27. Simon Chan, *Liturgical Theology: The Church as Worshiping Community* (Downers
Grove, Ill.: IVP Academic, 2006), p. 14.

Christian piety, they would run to "the riches of the Reformed, Lutheran, and Anglican traditions where these matters have been defined and articulated" and where worship "lies at the heart of the church's mission."[28] Such a return seems unlikely. As James White cautions his colleagues in liturgical studies, "Large segments of North American Christianity have no interest in ecumenism and are doing quite well without us."[29] In so doing, White establishes a dichotomy: ecumenical churches on one side, and pragmatic, evangelistically concerned "Frontier" churches on the other.

White's instinct that the explosive popularity of "seeker services" and the "church growth" movement of the 1980s were not new but had origins in nineteenth-century American revivalism was prescient. His analysis of the Frontier tradition in *Protestant Worship* (1989) anticipated influential popular and scholarly monographs of the late twentieth century, including Sally Morgenthaler's *Worship Evangelism* (1995), Rick Warren's *The Purpose-Driven Church* (1995), and Gregory Pritchard's *Willow Creek Seeker Services: Evaluating a New Way of Doing Church* (1996). Baffled and alarmed by the new evangelical worship trends infiltrating their denominations, mainline liturgical scholars increasingly relied on White's analysis to shape their critiques and conclusions.

My concern is that White's assessment represents a highly selective reading of the evangelical tradition, one that is more interested in the movement's discontinuities from historic Christianity than its ecumenical contributions. This lopsidedness can be attributed to the fact that liturgical historians and theologians seldom move beyond Charles Finney's *Lectures on Revivals of Religion* to probe how evangelical theology and practice had either developed before that work or matured in the 175 years since its publication. Paul Bradshaw offers an apt summary of the situation:

> The evidence presented by liturgical practice has often been misused by theologians, and the process has become no more than the equivalent of the practice of biblical proof texting. One determines *a priori* what doc-

---

28. D. G. Hart, "Why Evangelicals Think They Hate Liturgy," *Modern Reformation* 5 (1996): 20.

29. James White, "How Do We Know It Is Us?," in *Liturgy and the Moral Self*, ed. E. Byron Anderson and Bruce T. Morrill (Collegeville, Minn.: Liturgical Press, 1998), p. 58.

trinal position one espouses, and then quarries ancient liturgical texts in order to find material that could be interpreted in support of that position, sometimes without regard for the history of the text in question or its broader context in the rite.[30]

It is not unreasonable to speculate that White and his colleagues began with *a priori* judgments about the new megachurches (moralistic, pragmatic, anti-ecumenical) and then worked backward to Finney's writings as evidence for their conclusions.

But as ethicist Ted Smith points out, Finney's "new measures" cannot be confined to megachurches. They have indelibly shaped the rhetoric of preachers as diverse as William Sloane Coffin, T. D. Jakes, Rick Warren, and Barbara Brown Taylor.[31] According to Smith, "if details of techniques like the anxious bench exist only in echoes, the structures of practices like closing sermons with demands for decision remain widespread."[32] While some sermons might "ask people to make a decision to accept Christ as savior," others entreat the congregation to "live their best lives now, join a march against an imperialist war, commit themselves more fully to liturgical practices, or contribute to the capital campaign."[33] In short, Charles Finney's influence is ubiquitous and spans the evangelical/liturgical divide. It cannot be contained by, credited to, or blamed upon any single sector of Protestantism.

A second, more significant problem for Smith is the fact that when theologians read history, their first impulse is to separate the wheat from the chaff. This means theological histories are frequently dominated by narratives of decline: they begin by relating the historical past to a norm and then proceed to drive the story toward the present as a time of ruins.[34] The problem behind this methodology is that simple narratives of decline ignore "the messiness of history, where living communities and practices bring gifts and problems, sources of justice and injustice."[35] Indeed, theological histories

---

30. Paul Bradshaw, "Difficulties in Doing Liturgical Theology," *Pacifica* 11 (1998): 187.

31. Ted A. Smith, *The New Measures: A Theological History of Democratic Practice* (Cambridge: Cambridge University Press, 2007), p. 9.

32. Smith, *The New Measures*, p. 8.

33. Smith, *The New Measures*, p. 9.

34. Smith, *The New Measures*, p. 11.

35. Smith, *The New Measures*, p. 13.

"end in nihilism if we assume that any church practice that came to being in time is nothing more than a human invention, driven by interests, and so a fall away from the will of God."[36] This is not to say that "whatever is, is right" or that any church practice can become "simply and perfectly identical to the work of God in the world."[37] Instead, Smith (along with church historian David D. Daniels III) invites scholars to cultivate a perspective that is simultaneously historical and eschatological:

> Church practices hope for ends beyond what they actually accomplish. They point towards a horizon of redemption that they do not achieve in themselves. That horizon judges them, even as it is their glory. A theological history will remember both the judgment and the glory. It will remember how church practices came into being even as it remembers their hope for their redemption. It will be not only genetic, but also eschatological.[38]

The pragmatism of Charles Finney is but one historical piece of the evangelical worship story. A robust, eschatological history of the Frontier tradition must also account for the ecumenical legacy of Finney's predecessor, George Whitefield.

The Ecumenism of George Whitefield

George Whitefield (1714-1770) made seven tours of the American colonies, earning him the title of "Grand Itinerant." Everywhere Whitefield went, he spoke to crowds of unprecedented sizes. Some 10,000 people reportedly flocked to hear him in Philadelphia in 1741, and his farewell sermon in Bos- ton drew a crowd estimated between 23,000 and 30,000 people. The magnitude of this crowd can be more fully appreciated by noting that Boston's total population at the time was only about 20,000. Whitefield, a born actor,

36. Ted Smith, in David D. Daniels III and Ted A. Smith, "History, Practice, and Theological Education," in *For Life Abundant: Practical Theology, Theological Education, and Christian Ministry,* ed. Dorothy C. Bass and Craig Dykstra (Grand Rapids: Wm. B. Eerdmans, 2008), p. 220.

37. Smith, in Daniels and Smith, "History, Practice, and Theological Education," p. 220.

38. Smith, in Daniels and Smith, "History, Practice, and Theological Education," p. 220.

made revolutionary changes to colonial preaching by adopting methods of the stage. By all accounts, Whitefield was a powerful orator. In an age long before electronic amplification, his friend Benjamin Franklin estimated that Whitefield's voice could reach 30,000 hearers. Not only were the volume and clarity of Whitefield's voice exceptional; so was the expressive quality of his delivery. David Garrick, the most famous English actor of the eighteenth century, once reported that Whitefield could melt an audience simply by pronouncing the word "Mesopotamia." "I would give a hundred guineas if I could say 'Oh' like Mr. Whitefield," Garrick once sighed.[39]

Whitefield used the Bible as a theatrical "script" and was partial to Scripture passages that centered on a narrative or dialogue that he could expand. What thoughts were running through Abraham's head when the angel told him to sacrifice Isaac? How did Zacchaeus feel as he scrambled up the sycamore tree to better see Jesus? Whitefield blurred the line between church and theater by impersonating biblical characters and enacting their emotions with dramatic gestures and variations in voice. Especially amazing to his audiences was the fact that Whitefield spoke extemporaneously. Prior to Whitefield's arrival in America, colonial preachers wrote out their sermons and read them verbatim to congregations. Whitefield instead urged aspiring ministers to "preach without notes" and criticized recorded sermons as a deficiency in faith.[40]

Whitefield was a master not only of performance, but also of publicity: he was, in Frank Lambert's apt phrase, "a pioneer in the commercialization of religion."[41] Whitefield masterfully exploited technologies that had been unavailable in previous centuries, including highways and mail services. He sent copies of his itineraries in advance, making him a celebrity even before he arrived in a town or village. Along with his press agent, William Seward, he authored "puff pieces" for secular papers that extolled his successes; and in the year 1740, colonial newspapers from South Carolina to Pennsylvania devoted anywhere from one-third to two-thirds of their available space to

39. Harry S. Stout, *The Divine Dramatist: George Whitefield and the Rise of Modern Evangelicalism* (Grand Rapids: Wm. B. Eerdmans, 1991), p. 237.

40. Harry S. Stout, *The New England Soul: Preaching and Religious Culture in Colonial New England* (New York: Oxford University Press, 1986), p. 192.

41. Frank Lambert, *"Pedlar in Divinity": George Whitefield and the Transatlantic Revivals, 1737-1770* (Princeton: Princeton University Press, 1994), p. 9.

news about Whitefield. The evangelist also published sermons, a journal, and other works (often in multiple editions) to spread his fame: again in 1740, Lambert points out, Whitefield either authored or inspired 30 percent of all titles published in the American colonies.[42] The effects of this publicity were profound: Whitefield could influence people in more than one place at a time. People could purchase his printed works, read one of his sermons, or follow the many pamphlet debates being waged between Whitefield's supporters and his detractors. Critics might easily fold Whitefield's use of theatrics and media into a narrative of decline. But to fully understand the history of evangelical worship, we must press Ted Smith's question: What was the horizon of redemption toward which these new measures pointed?

We can find important clues by considering the historical context in which Whitefield lived and worked. From the beginning, Christians have affirmed their belief in the one, holy, catholic, and apostolic church. However, the mutual anathema between the Eastern and Western churches in the eleventh century, radical movements of dissent within Catholicism during the twelfth century, and the splintering of Reformed, Lutheran, Anglican, and Anabaptist churches from one another and Roman Catholicism during the sixteenth century all contributed to breaking the visible unity of the church.

The ecclesiological crisis came to a violent head in the seventeenth century: Reginald Ward rightly observes that the Thirty Years' War (1618-1648) was the closest Europe ever came to "confessional Armageddon."[43] During this tumultuous period, mainly Catholic armies opposed mainly Protestant armies for not-very-clear purposes, wreaking destruction that Europe had not seen since the Black Plague two and a half centuries earlier.[44] The Holy Roman Empire could no longer be held together and was divided into roughly three hundred principalities, bishoprics, and free cities. The loss of life was staggering, and the morale of Europe, along with the medieval dream of a unified Christendom, was shattered.

This is the historical context in which to understand the beginnings of modern evangelicalism. Bruce Hindmarsh explains that just as European

---

42. Lambert, *"Pedlar in Divinity,"* p. 6.

43. W. R. Ward, *Christianity under the Ancient Régime, 1648-1789* (Cambridge: Cambridge University Press, 1999), pp. 2-4.

44. Martin Marty, *The Christian World: A Global History* (New York: Modern Library, 2007), 119.

theology after the Second World War was profoundly chastened by the
memory of the compromises the church had made with National Social-
ism, so evangelical ecclesiology in the seventeenth and eighteenth centuries
"retain[ed] a vivid consciousness of an earlier religious holocaust."[45] The
writings of John Wesley offer a poignant illustration:

> [Wesley] looked back on the history of religious conflict in the previous
> century and saw it as a sad confirmation of innate human sinfulness.
> "There is a . . . horrid reproach to the Christian name, yea, to the name of
> man, to all reason and humanity," he lamented. "There is war in the world!
> War between men! War between Christians! I mean between those that
> bear the name of Christ and profess to 'walk as he also walked.'" Wesley
> deplored this religious violence associated with confessional politics. He
> urged instead a "catholic spirit," saying, "I ask not therefore of him with
> whom I would unite in love, 'Are you of my Church?'" Instead, he asked
> one question only: "Is thine heart right, as my heart is with thy heart?"[46]

George Whitefield shared his friend John Wesley's ecumenical ethos. Indeed, the very fact of their friendship was a testament to their "catholic
spirit," since the two Anglican ministers disagreed passionately and publicly over the issue of predestination. Whitefield once wrote, "I talk freely
with the Messrs. Wesley, though we widely differ in a certain point. Most
talk of a catholic spirit," he continued, "but it is only till they have brought
people into the pale of their own church. This is downright sectarianism,
not Catholicism. How can I act consistently, unless I receive and love all
the children of God, whom I esteem to be such, of whatever denomination
they may be?"[47]

In many ways, Whitefield lived out the principle of catholicity more
effectively than Wesley. Wesley gathered preachers around him and be-

---

45. Bruce Hindmarsh, "Is Evangelical Ecclesiology an Oxymoron? A Historical Perspective," in *Evangelical Ecclesiology: Reality or Illusion?*, ed. John G. Stackhouse Jr. (Grand Rapids:
Baker, 2003), p. 22.

46. John Wesley, "The Doctrine of Original Sin," in *The Works of the Reverend John Wesley*,
vol. 9, ed. Thomas Jackson (1872; reprint, Grand Rapids: Baker, 1984), p. 221.

47. Whitefield, quoted in Roger H. Martin, *Evangelicals United: Ecumenical Stirrings in
Pre-Victorian Britain, 1795-1830* (London: Scarecrow Press, 1983), p. 21.

gan a series of annual conferences with them, and these preachers in turn formed societies which came to be known as a "Connexion." As Roger Martin points out, the loyalty, cohesion, and discipline of Wesley's Connexion was comparable to the Jesuit order, and Wesley's control over it earned him the nickname "Pope John."[48] Indeed, the loyalty of the Connexion was such that "it effectively insulated Wesleyanism from any deep involvement with Christian societies beyond its fold."[49] By contrast, Whitefield was a roving evangelist. Between the years 1737 and 1770, he crossed the Atlantic Ocean thirteen times, making seven trips to America and voyages to Gibraltar and Bermuda, fifteen visits to Scotland, two journeys to Ireland, and two trips to Holland. "The whole world is now my parish," the Grand Itinerant declared in 1739.

If Wesley's genius was ecclesiastical organization, Whitefield's was ecclesiastical disruption. He crossed parochial boundaries of confessional and territorial Christendom, deliberately minimizing his connections to the Church of England and repeatedly raising the ire of the Anglican hierarchy. One Anglican minister deplored Whitefield's practice "of itinerating over all Parts of the British Dominions" and his readiness "to preach the Gospel to any Sect, Part, or Faction, that shew Willingness or Desire to hear [him]."[50] Another minister prohibited Whitefield from preaching in his pulpit on account of the itinerant's "frequent changing Sides (In one Country he is a true Son of the Church of England, in a second a stanch [sic] Presbyterian, and in a third, a strong Congregationalist)."[51]

Whitefield's response to these accusations was simple and straightforward. When an Anglican minister in Boston insisted that the Church of England was the only true church, Whitefield protested that he "saw regenerate souls among the Baptists, among the Presbyterians, among the Independents, and among the Church [i.e., Anglican] folks — all children of God, and yet all born again in a different way of worship." "Who can tell which is the most evangelical?" Whitefield queried.[52] Whitefield severely

48. Martin, *Evangelicals United*, p. 10.

49. Martin, *Evangelicals United*, p. 10.

50. Chris Beneke, *Beyond Toleration: The Religious Origins of American Pluralism* (New York: Oxford University Press, 2006), p. 55.

51. Beneke, *Beyond Toleration*, pp. 55-56.

52. Whitefield, quoted in Beneke, *Beyond Toleration*, p. 56.

antagonized the Boston clergy by claiming that he preferred "to preach up the new birth, and the power of godliness, and not to insist so much upon the form: for people would never be brought to one mind as to that; nor did Jesus Christ ever intend it."[53]

Herein lies a defining characteristic of contemporary evangelicalism: the de-emphasis of denominationalism to better serve the priority of the new birth.[54] Whitefield recognized early on that "one could regard church order as essential, as the Protestant Orthodox did, or one could regard regeneration by the Holy Spirit as essential, as evangelicals did, but one could not do both." Although evangelicals of Whitefield's day did not work out a distinctive doctrine of church order, they "seemed to see in their wider fellowship a manifestation of the mystical Church, discernible among the divided visible churches."[55] Thus, when Whitefield looked out across his massive audiences, he saw only two kinds of people: those who were converted and those who were not. One of Whitefield's sermons makes this clear: "It is very remarkable, there are but two sorts of people mentioned in Scripture: it does not say the Baptists and Independents, nor the Methodists and Presbyterians; no, Jesus Christ divides the whole world into but two classes, sheep and goats."[56] The very terminology of "new birth" encouraged listeners to identify themselves less with a particular denomination and more with the larger ecumenical Christian family. Whitefield brought home his point in typically dramatic fashion from a balcony in Philadelphia:

> Father Abraham, whom have you in heaven? Any Episcopalians? No! Any Presbyterians? No! Have you any Independents or Seceders? No! Have you any Methodists? No! No! No! Whom have you there? We don't know those names here! All who are here are Christians.[57]

53. See Roger Finke and Rodney Stark, *The Churching of America, 1776-1990* (New Brunswick: Rutgers University Press, 1992), p. 199.

54. See Thomas S. Kidd, *The Great Awakening: The Roots of Evangelical Christianity in Colonial America* (New Haven: Yale University Press, 2007), p. 40.

55. Hindmarsh, "Is Evangelical Ecclesiology an Oxymoron?," p. 32.

56. Whitefield, quoted in Jerome Dean Mahaffey, *Preaching Politics: The Religious Rhetoric of George Whitefield and the Founding of a New Nation* (Waco: Baylor University Press, 2007), p. 75.

57. Whitefield, quoted in Mahaffey, *Preaching Politics*, p. 76.

In this same vein, Whitefield once declared, "I wish all names of the saints of God were swallowed up in that one of *Christian*. I long for professors to leave off placing religion in saying, 'I am a church man,' 'I am a dissenter.' My language to such is, 'Are you of Christ? If so, I love you with all my heart.'"[58]

Whitefield was not interested in self-perpetuation or the creation of a new denomination: "I know my place . . . even to be the servant of all. I want not to have a people called after my name." He rejected the solution of earlier reformers who encouraged their followers to withdraw from "corrupt" denominations in order to form a "purer" sect.[59] Whitefield's intent was to sidestep, not supplant, existing churches by creating larger, translocal associations. As Harry Stout explains, these evangelical associations would be "purely voluntary and would allow people to remain in their favorite denomination even as they bound themselves to a large association with internal significance."[60] The unity of the early evangelical movement was not sacramental, nor did it have to do with authorized orders, forms, or rites: evangelicals disagreed sharply among themselves over these and other issues. Instead, "the principle by which unity was discerned was evangelical piety itself."[61] Stout sums up the position well: "If there was no new denomination with a capital letter reflecting its establishment, the New Birth itself assumed capital letters as the institutional and theological embodiment of a new religious movement."[62]

Whitefield helped to instantiate a new ecclesial consciousness in the modern world, one that seemed "to manifest temporarily the underlying unity of the children of God and to express this in various extra-ecclesial settings."[63] As Martin Marty explains, this evangelical ethos would radically redefine traditional American denominational lines in the twentieth century:

Foreign visitors come to the United States and expect to find that denominations which have given shape to Protestantism will also serve to define

---

58. Whitefield, quoted in Hindmarsh, "Is Evangelical Ecclesiology an Oxymoron?," p. 33.

59. Arnold Dallimore, *George Whitefield: The Life and Times of the Great Evangelist of the Eighteenth-Century Revival* (London: Banner of Truth Trust, 1970), vol. 2, p. 257.

60. Stout, *The New England Soul,* p. 204.

61. Hindmarsh, "Is Evangelical Ecclesiology an Oxymoron?," p. 15.

62. Stout, *The New England Soul,* p. 206.

63. Hindmarsh, "Is Evangelical Ecclesiology an Oxymoron?," p. 36.

its parties. Matters are not so easy as that. They may come across an Episcopalian and a Congregationalist. Their European textbooks, drawn from the doctrinal statements of these men's church bodies, will lead them to anticipate that what really separates these is that one believes in apostolic succession of bishops while the other stresses congregationalist order, or that one has a "catholic" view of the Lord's Supper and the other has a "free-church" view. [The European] may not have been misled about the nominal differences. But he will soon find that the two have more in common with each other on almost every other topic than either may have with another Episcopalian or another Congregationalist.[64]

Marty argues that ever since the fundamentalist-liberal controversies of the early twentieth century, American Protestantism has adopted a "two party system" mirroring the American political system. Theological and sociological issues have split every denomination into camps of "liberal" and "conservative" — a label that becomes more important to an individual's theological identity than that of a particular denomination. However, the seeds of this controversy were planted well before the twentieth century: as early as the 1730s and 1740s, "New Light" Anglican evangelicals were finding common cause with like-minded Congregationalists, Presbyterians, and Dutch Reformed, even as anti–New Light Presbyterians forged alliances with anti–New Light Anglicans, Dutch Reformed, and Congregationalists.[65] This is a paradox of Whitefield's legacy: evangelicalism draws together people of different churches while dividing those within the same denomination.

Continuing Questions

One unresolved issue that the Frontier tradition has inherited from Whitefield is a question about the necessity of denominations. Many evangelicals have turned Whitefield's vision of ecumenism rooted in the experience of

64. Martin E. Marty, *Righteous Empire: The Protestant Experience in America* (New York: Dial Press, 1970), p. 179.

65. See Beneke, *Beyond Toleration*, pp. 81-82.

New Birth into a new ecclesiological principle; indeed, sociologists have identified the growth of nondenominational Protestantism as one of the most significant developments in American religion in the past fifty years.[66] These Christians make a conscious decision not to affiliate with churches that are part of a denomination. The pastor of a megachurch in Nashville explains the demographic of his congregation this way:

> There's so many people here that, if somebody else asked what denomina-
> tion they are, they might still say Baptist or Lutheran or whatever, because
> that's where they still feel their roots are, but they attend church here, and
> it's just a part of the body of Christ — we're not big on the label thing.[67]

Of course, as Nancy Ammerman points out, the very act of refusing an external denominational label can result in high levels of commitment. She suggests that just as "claiming a Catholic or Lutheran identity provides a recognizable place on the religious map, we are now recognizing the space occupied by nondenominational churches and according it a kind of iron-ically 'denominational' identity."[68] From this perspective, Frontier Chris-tianity is best understood independently: it stands side-by-side with other Protestant traditions as a "nondenominational denomination," so to speak.

While some evangelicals endorse this approach, others find the confes-sional fluidity of nondenominationalism problematic. For example, William Dyrness is troubled by evangelical expressions of the church that "[refuse] to believe they are products of anything except the Bible" and will not call their groupings of churches "denominations."[69] Denominations, Dyrness argues, "embody the historical traditions that, for better or worse, have made Chris-tianity what it is."[70] Richard Mouw, a self-identified "evangelical Calvinist," voices a similar concern:

66. Corwin E. Smidt, *Pulpit and Politics: Clergy in American Politics at the Advent of the Millennium* (Waco: Baylor University Press, 2004), p. 285.

67. Quoted in Nancy T. Ammerman, *Pillars of Faith: American Congregations and Their Partners* (Berkeley and Los Angeles: University of California Press, 2005), p. 217.

68. Ammerman, *Pillars of Faith,* p. 217.

69. William A. Dyrness, "Spaces for an Evangelical Ecclesiology," in *Community of the Word* (Downers Grove, Ill.: InterVarsity Press, 2005), p. 261.

70. Dyrness, "Spaces for an Evangelical Ecclesiology," p. 261.

I am not happy when people treat "fundamentalism" and "evangelical-ism" as labels that refer to theological perspectives in the same way as "Lutheranism" and "Orthodox" do. I think "evangelical" is best thought of as a theological modifier rather than as a noun. The label should not be allowed to stand alone when sorting out theological systems.[71]

Like Dyrness, Mouw worries about the rise of "a generic evangelicalism that sees itself as an alternative to all other confessions."[72] Seen from this per-spective, Frontier Christianity is best understood in symbiotic relationship with other Protestant liturgical traditions: it does not need to be singled out for special analytical treatment. Robert Webber explains:

> The liturgy becomes a retelling and reliving of the evangelical experi-ence and conviction. When evangelicals sing the *Gloria in Excelsis Deo,* confess their sin, listen to the Word proclaimed and preached, recite the Creed, pray the intercessory prayer, pass the Kiss of Peace, sing the *Sanc-tus,* proclaim the mystery, and walk forward to eat the bread and drink the wine, they do so out of experience. What the liturgy says and does the evangelical has experienced — and experiences again every time the liturgy is done.[73]

Of course, many liturgical scholars worry that the evangelical/liturgical relationship is more parasitic than it is symbiotic. Maxwell Johnson and Frank Senn offer examples from a Lutheran perspective. Senn observes that a denominational church might hold both "traditional" and "contemporary" services every Sunday morning. The "traditional" service usually relies upon a book of worship and a hymnal — official denominational resources that are authorized only after lengthy formal review processes. That same con-

71. Richard J. Mouw, "What Evangelicals Can Learn from Fundamentalists," in *Pilgrims on the Sawdust Trail: Evangelical Ecumenism and the Quest for Christian Identity,* ed. Timothy George (Grand Rapids: Baker, 2004), p. 72.

72. Richard J. Mouw, "The Problem of Authority in Evangelical Christianity," in *Church Unity and the Papal Office,* ed. Carl E. Braaten and Robert W. Jenson (Grand Rapids: Wm. B. Eerdmans, 2001), p. 141.

73. Robert E. Webber, *Evangelicals on the Canterbury Trail: Why Evangelicals Are At-tracted to the Liturgical Church* (Waco: Word Books, 1985), p. 169.

gregation's "contemporary" service might depend upon products from an independent publisher that have not been reviewed by official liturgical commissions. Senn notes this as an area of concern. Johnson offers this related caution:

> What we do or don't do in our liturgies forms the community in one way or another. Hence, a [Lutheran] community which celebrates and receives Christ's Body and Blood in the Lord's Supper every Sunday, attends to the rubrical options and varieties already present in the "authorized" liturgical book(s), faithfully proclaims the lectionary readings, and tenaciously keeps the feasts and seasons of the liturgical year week after week, year after year, will be a different sort of community than one which is continually experimenting with "worship alternatives" and searching for something "better" to meet the so-called "needs" of worshippers and potential seekers alike. And I dare say that the first type of community will, undoubtedly, be more "orthodox," more "Lutheran," in its doctrinal-theological outlook.[74]

"Put somewhat crassly," he concludes, "if we want 'Lutheran' believers, we form and inform our congregations with 'Lutheran' liturgy."[75]

It makes theological and methodological sense for liturgical scholars in mainline Protestant traditions to examine the "contemporary" or "seeker" services in their denominations and query whether the content is "really Lutheran" or "authentically Presbyterian" (to cite but two possible examples). However, this line of questioning is less helpful when analyzing the worship of churches like the one I will introduce in the next chapter. Because they do not have a central liturgical commission, there is no tension in these churches about using "unauthorized" versus "authorized" denominational resources. Furthermore, the current scholarly shorthand for describing worship in these churches as "preliminaries" or "warm-up" is both pejorative and outdated. The *ordo* that characterized Finney's revival services no longer neatly maps

---

74. Maxwell Johnson, "Is Anything Normative in Contemporary Lutheran Worship?," in *The Serious Business of Worship: Essays in Honour of Bryan D. Spinks,* ed. Melanie Ross and Simon Jones (London: T&T Clark International, 2010), p. 177.

75. Johnson, "Is Anything Normative in Contemporary Lutheran Worship?," p. 179.

onto current worship practices because the popularity of the "seeker service" model has waned markedly among evangelicals in recent years.[76] New categories of liturgical-theological analysis need to be cultivated.

Conclusion

Liturgical scholars frequently establish a dichotomy between ecumenical churches and Frontier-*ordo* churches, often enjoining the latter to be more like the former. Ecumenist Eugene Brand's observation is representative: "Most of us liturgists work either as if [Baptist, Pentecostal, charismatic, and conservative evangelical churches] did not exist, or we are prepared to tolerate them benignly until they are prepared to enter our convergence."[77] Despite his insistence that the historian's role is merely to describe practices that persist in liturgical communities without passing judgment,[78] James White is unapologetic in making similar evaluative claims: "It is time for [evangelicals] to acknowledge that church growth must be growth in depth as well as in numbers." They must "make a serious commitment to worship reform and not leave it to Roman Catholics and other Protestants. . . . The time is now; no further hesitation can be excused."[79]

It is tempting to conclude in a similar vein, bringing the questions raised in this chapter to resolution with prescriptive directives. Instead, I join Ted Smith in urging liturgical theologians to move beyond simple narratives of progress and decline. Narratives of progress and decline have grown to feel natural: the simple fact of their familiarity gives them a kind of authority. By contrast, Smith points out, "the ironies of redemption do not fit easily into narratives of progress or decline. But they come to life in stories told from the standpoint of hope."[80] Smith's words are not a validation of the triumphalism that has come from some corners of the Frontier tradition:

76. See "Willow Creek's 'Huge Shift,'" *Christianity Today* 52, no. 6 (2008): 13.

77. Eugene Brand, "Berakah Response: Ecumenism and the Liturgy," *Worship* 58 (1984): 312.

78. White, *Protestant Worship*, p. 15.

79. White, "The Missing Jewel of the Evangelical Church," *The Reformed Journal*, June 1986, pp. 15-16.

80. Smith, *The New Measures*, p. 13.

claims, for example, that liturgical forms and styles were "dying on the brink of the twenty-first century,"[81] or that new evangelical experiments in worship carried with them "all the conceptual and theological underpinnings necessary for longevity."[82] Indeed, Smith issues a sobering warning on this front:

> The new measures do not unroll easily toward some normatively charged end. . . . If their stories are to be told with moral and theological significance, they will have to be told from the perspective of an end they do not reach on their own, a standpoint occupied now only in hope. For if they are to be redeemed, their redemption will come neither from a little more progress on the road they are already on, nor from a quick reversal to retrace their steps and then run in the other direction. It will come in death and resurrection, or not at all.[83]

Bearing Smith's caution in mind, I conclude by taking up an invitation extended by Michael Aune in his review of James White's *Protestant Worship:* "An interesting way to gauge whether White has been successful in his assessment of Protestant worship might be to ask a variety of folks whose traditions these are whether he has indeed captured their 'genius' or 'ethos.'"[84] This chapter's re-examination of the Frontier tradition suggests the answer to Aune's question is both yes and no. The strength of White's account is its proper emphasis on evangelism and pragmatism as driving forces of the evangelical movement. The weakness of White's account is its misleading suggestion that evangelicals have focused their energies on these things at the expense of ecumenism. Pragmatism and ecumenism function in the Frontier tradition not as a dichotomy, but as a dialectic of hope and history. At its best, Frontier worship succeeds brilliantly in uniting evangelicals across denominations. At its worst, Frontier worship continues to stir up contentious intradenominational disputes. This is the mixed field of wheat and tares that evangelicals have inherited from Whitefield and Finney, and it sets the scene for the case study to follow.

81. Bill Easum and Thomas Bandy, *Growing Spiritual Redwoods* (Nashville: Abingdon Press, 1997), p. 70.

82. Easum and Bandy, *Growing Spiritual Redwoods,* p. 283.

83. Smith, *The New Measures,* p. 12.

84. Michael B. Aune, "Protestant Worship: Traditions in Transition," *Theological Studies* 51 (1990): 792.

CHAPTER TWO

Case Study 1:
Eastbrook Church

Have you ever wondered how it would be to have someone next to you kneeling in the aisle while you are standing and praying? Do you ever wonder how it would be to have foreign languages sung, prayed, and shouted as you listen in your limited English? Have you ever seen someone in an ethnic robe, with their eyes focused on something ethereal and unseen? Does your heart soften when you are welcomed by the people around you and leap when the worship team greets you with a joy-filled "Good Morning"? There is something unique to be had at every service.

Margaret, congregation member, Eastbrook Church

Worship at Eastbrook: A Snapshot

It is several minutes before the official eleven A.M. start time, and worship at Eastbrook Church is already well under way. A brass ensemble of three trumpets, three trombones, and two horns form a makeshift orchestra pit at the front of a wooden stage. Forty or so choir members are assembled on risers: their faces — a rich blend of colors and skin tones — are a microcosmic representation of the congregation as a whole. The choir and orchestra have first-generation immigrants from Nigeria, Brazil, Germany, Russia, and France; in fact, approximately one-third of Eastbrook's members are minorities from seventy different ethnic groups. As one member commented to me,

"When I look at our congregation worshiping together, I sometimes think to myself, 'This is a picture of heaven! All the nations coming together to sing to the Lord!'" It was a sentiment echoed repeatedly throughout my study.

Now a woman in front of me tucks her G.E.D. study guide and her Bible underneath a chair. "Send it on down! Send it on down!/Lord, let the Holy Ghost come on down!" the choir exclaims in four-part harmony. Their joy is palpable and infectious, and the congregation responds by tapping its toes, raising its hands, and sending up encouraging amens.

At the conclusion of the call to worship, Marc, the senior pastor, offers a short word of prayer: "Holy Spirit, we know that you hear our prayers, and we pray that you would come down just as we've asked. Sometimes we don't realize that you might change us radically and make us uncomfortable. But we want you to be free to do that. Change us as we worship this morning; fall fresh upon all the churches across the city today. We ask it in Jesus' name. Amen." After Marc finishes praying, brass, piano, organ, and timpani sound a familiar introduction. The congregation sings together, first in English, then in Spanish:

> Holy, holy, holy! Lord God Almighty!
> Early in the morning our song shall rise to Thee;
> Holy, holy, holy! Merciful and mighty!
> God in three persons, blessed Trinity!

English

> ¡Santo, ¡Santo, ¡Santo! Señor omnipotente!
> Siempre el labio mío loores te dará.
> ¡Santo, ¡Santo, ¡Santo! Te adoro reverente!
> Dios en tres personas, bendita Trinidad.

Spanish

The instrumentalists make a seamless transition to a lilting gospel style. Tambourines replace timpani as the congregation begins a new chorus: "Worthy to receive glory;/worthy to receive honor;/worthy to receive all our praise today./Praise him! Praise him and lift him up!/Praise him! Exalt his name forever!"[1] Next comes the more reflective "Revelation Song," which continues the morning's eschatological theme: "Worthy is the Lamb who was

1. Gary Oliver, "Holy, Holy, Holy" (High Praises, 1991).

slain;/holy, holy is he./Sing a new song to him who sits on/heaven's mercy seat./Holy, holy, holy is the Lord God Almighty/who was and is and is to come."[2] At the conclusion of the songs, a worship leader steps forward with a prayer of confession and repentance:

> Lord, we know that you are indeed holy, and exalted, and seated on the throne. We can't even begin to imagine how glorious you really are. As we stand in contrast, we realize how filthy the rags are that we put on ourselves. We come before you this morning as a body of believers, asking to be forgiven corporately. This city would be turned on its head if we as a church were doing what we are called to be doing by you. And we're not. We sometimes think that what goes on within these four walls is far more important to us than what happens beyond them. Lord, you called us to a world that's dying, and we as a people have failed you. Please forgive us.
>
> We also come to you as individuals. We can't seem to let go of all you've given us. We even call it our own — "it's mine" or "it's ours" — and it's not. It's yours. You give it to us as stewards to further your kingdom. Lord, change our minds, and change our hearts. Get our eyes off of ourselves. Please forgive us. Thank you, God, that you promise to be faithful and forgive us when we confess our sins. We ask that you would make us more and more into the image of your Son, Jesus, this week and right now. We pray it all in Jesus' name. Amen.

The congregation responds with a sung prayer of confession: "Living God, Consuming Fire,/burn the sin from my life./Make your will my desire,/take my life in your hands./Purify me with your love/till I shine far brighter/than purest gold in your eyes."[3]

The worship leader steps forward again, this time to offer intercessory prayer. He names specific families struggling with health concerns or experiencing bereavement and prays in general for all those in the congregation struggling with depression, the loss of a home, or unemployment. He also highlights the names of the church's missionaries, the city of Milwaukee and each of its suburbs, the nations of Iran, Iraq, Lebanon, Israel, and all places

2. Jennie Lee Riddle, "Revelation Song" (Gateway Create Publishing, 2004).
3. Annie Herring, "Purify Me" (Latter Rain Music, 1988).

in need of God's peace. At the conclusion of his prayer, the choir sings "O Clap Your Hands," a setting of Psalm 47 arranged for choir, organ, brass, and percussion by Ralph Vaughan Williams. The anthem is jubilant and technically complex; after the tithes and offerings have been collected, the congregation responds with appreciative applause. The church sings a final song together as children are dismissed to their Sunday school classes and the choir files off the stage.

Pastor Marc is in the middle of a sermon series on the Holy Spirit, and this morning he begins with an anecdote:

> When my family and I were in Ethiopia as missionaries, getting ready to move to Somalia, the ambassador said to me, "You'll like Bulo Burti (a town whose name means 'dust village') because the wind always blows there." Sure enough, when we got to Somalia, there were days when the temperature was 110 degrees, and in some places the wind didn't blow at all. It was unbelievably hot and unbearable. But when the wind would come, you would forget because it would cool you. When there was rain, the wind came first. That's the picture God gives us of himself: that in a place that is intolerable without him, the Spirit is the harbinger of life.

A few minutes later, Marc warms to one of his favorite biblical passages. He reads the first three verses of Ezekiel 37 to the congregation:

> The hand of the Lord was upon me, and he brought me out by the Spirit of the Lord and set me in the middle of a valley; it was full of bones. He led me back and forth among them, and I saw a great many bones on the floor of the valley, bones that were very dry. He asked me, "Son of man, can these bones live?" I said, "O Sovereign LORD, you alone know."

"If you want a good understanding of the world from God's perspective, it's a valley of dead bones," Marc explains. His voice crescendos as he continues:

> Have you walked around your neighborhood, or around the city, and just seen all the dry, empty, and lifeless people? Have you ever asked yourself if Milwaukee can really live? Can God do anything about this? If you have a puny idea of God — if he comes and stirs things up and makes

you feel good every once in a while — then the answer is "No." But if the Holy Spirit is a driving wind from God that is everywhere, beyond time, in time, of time — if the Holy Spirit is someone who is completely other than us who has the power to do anything in creation — then the answer is "Yes!" God has the power to take dead people like us and give us new birth, and bring us to life.

After several minutes, he continues reading from Ezekiel:

> And as I was prophesying, there was a noise, a rattling sound, and the bones came together, bone to bone. I looked, and tendons and flesh appeared on them and skin covered them, but there was no breath in them. Then he said to me, "Prophesy to the breath; prophesy, son of man, and say to it, 'This is what the Sovereign LORD says: Come from the four winds, O breath, and breathe into these slain, that they may live.'" So I prophesied as he commanded me, and breath entered them; they came to life and stood up on their feet — a vast army.

This, Marc suggests, is a picture of the church: God wants the Spirit to enter into the people, so that they become, by his presence, the people of God.

Later in the sermon, Marc connects Ezekiel 37 with Ephesians 2:21-22: "In [Christ] the whole building is joined together and rises to become a holy temple in the Lord. And in him you too are being built together to become a dwelling in which God lives by his Spirit." Marc reminds the congregation, "All there is of God was in Jesus Christ, who went to the cross to accomplish our salvation. And through the power of Christ's resurrection, through the Spirit, he puts all there is of God into the church so that we can be the temple of God right now." Marc emphasizes the meaning of "temple" here:

> The temple Paul talks about in Ephesians is not a Catholic temple. It's not a Lutheran temple, or a Protestant temple, or a nondenominational evangelical temple. No. The Spirit's power is immense. He not only holds the universe together physically; he also holds the church of Jesus Christ together with all its members and makes us one. The love that holds the Triune God together — Father, Son, and Holy Spirit — is the same powerful love that holds the church together. This love can be released in us

through the power of the Spirit and be brought to bear on our marriages, our families, our friends, neighbors, and co-workers, even our enemies. This is why we were put on earth.

The congregation responds with a song entitled "Spirit, Touch Your Church." The worship team sings the first stanza: "Lord, we humbly come before you./We don't deserve of you what we ask./But we yearn to see your glory;/restore this dying land." As the assembly catches the melody, it improvises harmony lines and joins in the reflective chorus: "Spirit, touch your church,/stir the hearts of men./Revive us, Lord,/with your passion once again./I want to care for others/like Jesus cares for me./Let your rain fall upon me."[4] Marc concludes the service with a brief prayer: "O God, please be the driving wind in us. Please be the breath of life that we can introduce to others. Let us be the fire of Christ for the world. We pray this in the name of the Father, the Son, and the Holy Spirit. Amen."

Historical and Demographical Background

Eastbrook's story begins at Elmbrook Church, a nondenominational, evangelical megachurch located in an affluent suburb in western Milwaukee. Since its founding in 1958, Elmbrook has grown to become the largest church in Wisconsin; a 2008 survey lists it as one of the hundred largest churches in the United States. In 1979, a group of individuals from Elmbrook felt called to establish a congregation on Milwaukee's east side. Marc Erickson — a physician who served as a medical missionary in Ethiopia and Somalia, chairman of the emergency department at a large Milwaukee hospital, and pastor to the college students at Elmbrook — was invited to be the church's first senior pastor. It is a position he continues to hold more than thirty years later.

Reflecting on Eastbrook's early days, Marc admits, "We had no clue how to start a church. We didn't read any books. Our organizational team had Communists, Republicans, and Democrats all around the table, and we had no idea how to take all the diverse ideas and reconcile them." He highlights an additional complicating factor:

4. Kim Bollinger, "Spirit, Touch Your Church" (copyright 1989 by Kim Bollinger).

I had been a college pastor. When Eastbrook started, I hadn't been to seminary, so there wasn't much difference between me and the people in the pews. I had no idea all the things that could go wrong. Everyone who came through our doors seemed to have a list of ten or fifteen problems — relational problems, emotional problems, theological problems — and we didn't know what to do. It dawned on me that we had not thought through how to start a church well enough. There was chaos, ignorance, a lack of experience, and no planning.

However, over the next five years, the young church began to find its feet. Eastbrook rented meeting space in a Milwaukee public school and established a lay counseling ministry, programs for children and youth, and a ministry to artists and musicians. A significant turning point came in 1984, when the vice president of Somalia asked Marc to rebuild a missionary hospital in the village of Bulo Burti — the site where he had served until the political upheaval of the 1970s forced all missionaries to flee. With very little discussion, the Eastbrook Church council voted unanimously to support the project. "This is one of the problems of inviting an emergency room doctor to be your senior pastor," Marc chuckles. "When emergencies hit — 'Bang!' — I have to take care of them immediately. If we had thought more about this, we would never have done it." The work was daunting: buildings that had sat abandoned for fifteen years were in desperate need of repair, and initially there was no clean water or electricity. Diesel fuel to run the emergency hospital generator was scarce. However, Eastbrook embraced the challenge. The congregation, which did not yet own its own facility, poured a quarter of a million dollars a year into East Africa. Thirty volunteers from the church rebuilt the hospital and changed the system of health care in the surrounding area until civil war forced the hospital to close permanently.

A second significant turning point in Eastbrook's history came in 1995, when the congregation purchased St. Nicholas Roman Catholic Church. Again, Marc stresses that Eastbrook had little idea what it was getting into at the time: "When we bought this building, it was [in] one of the highest crime areas of the city, and a drug drop center of the area. Gangs chopped up cars, and no one could go on the streets and not get robbed." Marc reports that St. Nicholas lost an average of two cars a week from their parking lot: local gangs made a game of stealing them out from under the eyes of the armed guards.

The neighborhood has changed dramatically in the last decade. Gang members have been arrested, crackhouses have been shut down, low-income housing has been remodeled, and crime levels have dropped significantly. The neighborhood is no longer on the police department's radar screen. Marc reports that in fifteen years, only two cars have been stolen from Eastbrook's parking lot, and both have been returned within an hour. Marc and his congregation attribute this turnaround completely to the power of prayer: "When we bought the building, we began praying in the sanctuary every Monday through Friday at six A.M. We haven't stopped praying since." One congregant who grew up on the outskirts of the neighborhood describes the transformation this way: "When I was young, we biked to the area. Gradually it became unsafe and violent, and we found other, more secure places to go. Today if someone dropped me off near the church, I would enjoy the walk. Eastbrook has opened a previously dark and dreary neighborhood to many and turned it into a pillar of light and promise — as only a place of God can."

From the outside, Eastbrook's 1950s blonde brick building still looks like a Roman Catholic church. Inside, however, the changes in architecture are pronounced. The oblong nave of St. Nicholas originally had a longitudinal orientation, with fixed pews facing a high altar in the eastern apse. However, Eastbrook has modified the space to better serve its needs. The altar has been removed, the apse has been filled with additional seating, and a stage has been constructed midway down the length of the northern wall. The nave has been carpeted and turned sideways, so to speak; moveable chairs are arranged in a large semicircle facing the stage. Two homemade vertical banners are displayed at each end of the sanctuary. The first shows multicolored hands reaching heavenward, ascending music notes, and the message "Jesus is Lord of All." The second banner declares "Proclaiming Salvation to All" and features abstract, multicolored persons dancing around a cross. Ten tall windows of leaded stained glass cover the length of the southern wall; during morning worship, soft light filters through their blue, green, yellow, and red geometric patterns and casts patterns on the floor behind the congregation. Ten shorter, identically patterned windows line the northern wall behind the stage; a large wooden cross also hangs on the wall. Projection screens hang on either side of the stage; on the floor beneath sits a grand piano, a drum set, and an electric organ.

Beneath the sanctuary is a large fellowship hall and kitchen. However, the most significant downstairs renovations are safely locked behind closed doors on Sunday mornings: Eastbrook has constructed five examination rooms in the basement of the church, including a complete optical room that boasts state-of-the-art equipment. Eastbrook is a partner in the Bread of Healing Clinics, a ministry started by a local Lutheran church to provide cost-free primary medical care to uninsured adults in the Milwaukee area. Every second and fourth Monday and every third Saturday of the month, the congregation opens its church doors wide, and an all-volunteer team of physicians, nurses, educators, pharmacists, and respiratory therapists tend to patients with chronic illnesses. According to the most recent statistics available, the clinic at Eastbrook serves about thirty ethnic groups and received a total of 572 visits in 2008. Many of these patients consider the church to be their primary medical home. Eastbrook also acts as a clearinghouse for medication distribution to other free clinics and community clinics.[5]

A short walk across the parking lot leads to Holy Grounds, the church's coffee shop. It is painted in warm colors, furnished with plush, overstuffed couches and wooden chairs and tables, and features photography exhibits by local artists. While church coffee shops with free wireless Internet are not unusual in the American landscape, the story of Holy Grounds is unique. Eastbrook's café began as Junior's Sports Bar and Grill — a neighborhood hangout that featured a big-screen TV, bar food specials, and live music on weekends. Over the years, Junior's acquired a reputation for noisy bikers, drug-dealing, and crime; in 1999, a former Milwaukee Bucks basketball star was held up at gunpoint outside the bar and robbed of $40,000 worth of valuables. The violence escalated in 2003, when three people were injured in a shooting near the bar. Outraged neighbors demanded the bar's closing, and the owner eventually agreed to sell the property to Eastbrook. The renovated shop now serves as an outreach to the community and a meeting space for fellowship and church business.

Eastbrook is an active presence in its neighborhood in many other ways. Every Saturday morning, the church distributes food and groceries to anyone in need. Its Neighborhood Learning Center, adjacent to the coffee shop, is bursting at the seams and currently working to add more hours. Here, volunteers tutor adults working toward their G.E.D.s and help students of all ages in math, reading, and basic computer skills.

5. The demographic information here comes from my 2010 study.

Food + groceries

In its early years, Eastbrook focused on sending missionaries to underserved corners of the world — a theological priority that continues today. The church sends missionaries to Africa, the Far East, Central Asia, the Middle East, Central America, and Eastern Europe; it supports them financially and sends short-term visiting work teams to offer practical help. As time went on, the church became increasingly aware that the nations were coming to the city of Milwaukee. Marc points to the international students in the city's university system:

> International students are extremely lonely people. Many of them get here and after a few months want to go home. If you go to the graduate level and you see these people learning English so they can pass their TOEFL [Test of English as a Foreign Language] exam, and if you could read what they're journaling, you would just stop what you're doing and get in your car and take them home. Immigrants feel the same way. People coming out of Central America feel the same way. So we as a church have discovered that, and we're learning and working at how to get together in each other's lives. It's not an easy thing. But it's worth the effort.

In keeping with this ethos, Eastbrook offers weekly courses in English as a Second Language at the church during the eleven-o'clock hour of Sunday worship and hosts Bible studies in Arabic, Chinese, Russian, Hindi, and African languages throughout the city. Every month, the church holds a "Global Gateway" potluck that features the food and language of a particular nation. There are approximately fifty to sixty nations represented in Eastbrook's congregation at any given time, and the church is passionate about encouraging diversity among believers and unity between all ethnic groups. One of the ways the church actively fosters these connections is through music. To cite one memorable example, a few years ago the church's worship pastor, Ruth, worked with an ethnomusicologist at a nearby university to set the lyrics of the hymn "In Christ There Is No East or West" to Chinese harmonies. The adult choir then spent several months working with a language tutor from the congregation in order to sing the verses in both English and Mandarin Chinese.

In the same year, the children's choirs also worked with volunteers from the church to learn native songs in Russian, Spanish, Somali, and Arabic languages. A pamphlet from children's ministries explains, "From the time they're told that God loves them, the children of Eastbrook church are also told that God loves the world too. It's an easy lesson to learn when you're squirming around in Sunday school class next to someone from Nigeria, Korea, China, Russia, the Middle East, or some other faraway part of the world brought close enough to giggle with and poke." One member emphasized, "The theology of this church is a picture of all of our adoption by God. In fact, the diversity of the church is one of the things that made my husband and I comfortable to adopt internationally: it's common for kids not to look like their parents around here."

Pastor Marc summarized his hope for Eastbrook this way:

> I think evangelicals are prone to think, "Well, I'm getting into heaven no matter what I do." So you look at our ethics, and you look at the performance of the evangelical church, and at times it's been pretty bad. It's a scandal. Not only that, but we've got other problems. We believe there's a sacred and a secular, which is just nonsense: when Christ comes to live within us, everything's sacred. We believe that the church is a building, which is foolishness. The church is us. We think that worship is one hour on Sunday, when worship is really everything we do. At Eastbrook, we try to stand up against these heresies, because if you believe worship is one hour a week, and if you believe that secular is one part of your day, and if you believe that the building is the church, then how are we ever going to change the city?

Theological Analysis

Worship at Eastbrook Church defies the dichotomy of pragmatism and ecumenism presented in the previous chapter. Chapter One noted that after Charles Finney, much of what happened in American worship became highly practical: "Do what works in worship." "One could speak of the Pragmatic Tradition instead of the Frontier Tradition," James White suggests.[6]

6. James F. White, "Worship and Evangelism from New Lebanon to Nashville," in *Christian Worship in North America: A Retrospective, 1955-1995,* ed. James F. White (Collegeville, Minn.: Liturgical Press, 1997), p. 159.

And indeed, certain components of Eastbrook's worship and ministry —
its optical examination room in the church basement, for example, and its
English language classes offered during Sunday morning worship — are
pragmatic in the best sense of the term. Eastbrook serves a complex urban
and international population; accordingly, it must raise questions of "Will
this work?" on a regular basis.

However, pragmatism is not the primary ethos guiding Eastbrook's worship decisions. (A Midwest church choir that devotes half a year to learning
a song in Mandarin Chinese clearly does not have pragmatism at the top of
its theological priority list!) Although the congregation is keenly interested
in evangelism, it does not subscribe to Finney's Frontier *ordo* of preliminary
songs that soften the heart, a fervent sermon, and the call for a personal
response. Instead, Eastbrook's philosophy-of-worship statement emphasizes
biblical components of worship that all churches share in common. It reads,
in part, as follows:

> We believe God created all people to worship Him, and He calls us —
> the body of Christ called Eastbrook Church — to worship Him together.
> Scripture teaches that worship includes singing psalms, hymns, and spiri-
> tual songs (Ephesians 5:19-20), thanksgiving (Psalm 35:18), confession and
> repentance (2 Chronicles 7:14; 1 John 1:9), giving of financial gifts (2 Co-
> rinthians 9:7-8) and tithes (Luke 11:42; Malachi 3:10), preaching of God's
> Word (1 Corinthians 14:24-25), [and] celebration of communion (1 Corin-
> thians 11:23-26). We follow this teaching by incorporating drama, dance,
> music (choral and instrumental), prayer, responsive scripture readings,
> testimonies, visual arts, and congregational singing into worship services.

How they do it

Dee, a charter member of the church and its first pastor of worship, explained
the service shape in an interview:

> The general shape of the service is twofold: God presents himself, and
> we respond. We come into God's presence, acknowledging and praising
> him. Seeing that God is so holy, we become aware of ourselves and our
> sin before him. So, next there needs to be a reflection on who we are
> as sinners before a holy God. We might bring that out either through
> song, Scripture, or prayer. Then we come to the assurance of God's pardon

— and again, the expression of that pardon could come through song, Scripture, or prayer. After we come past our tendency to sin, our ears are opened to hear the Word. So, then there's the sermon. After that, it's time for the offering — we are so grateful for God's word to us that we desire to respond. Isaiah 6 is a pattern we've used frequently to help us develop this understanding. At the end of the service, God asks, "Who will go for me? You've heard my Word; now who will go and tell others about who I am?" So we are sent out into the world, but not without a strong sense of worship within us. Worship does not begin and end with the Sunday morning service.

One member of the congregation summarized matters this way: "The worship that goes on here [in the sanctuary] puts a fire in us that carries us on to the other worship experience, which is what happens at work, or what happens at home, or what happens in any place you find yourself. It's all worship. How you do your job, or how you handle unemployment, or how you raise your kids at home, or how you plant your lilies in the backyard. *All of it* is worship."

This link between worship and ethics is a potentially rich site of connection between evangelical and liturgical traditions. In the previous century, the Liturgical Movement emphasized that true worship and sacramental participation should restore humanity to its true status in Christ, and that this should have a visible outworking in society.[7] More recently, Kevin Irwin has stressed that "praying *(lex orandi)* and believing *(lex credendi)* find their ultimate authentication in truly Christian living *(lex vivendi)*."[8] Don Saliers summarizes the matter succinctly: the issue is whether we can "pray what we mean and mean what we pray without being drawn into the way in which God views the world."[9]

The link between worship and ethics has become increasingly significant for many evangelicals. Perhaps the most striking example is the paradigm shift

---

7. See John Fenwick and Bryan Spinks, *Worship in Transition: The Liturgical Movement in the Twentieth Century* (New York: Continuum, 1995), pp. 10-11.

8. Kevin Irwin, *Models of the Eucharist* (Mahwah, N.J.: Paulist Press, 2005), p. x.

9. Don E. Saliers, "Liturgy and Ethics: Some New Beginnings," in *Liturgy and the Moral Self: Humanity at Full Stretch before God,* ed. E. Byron Anderson and Bruce T. Morrill (Collegeville, Minn.: Liturgical Press, 1998), p. 25.

of Sally Morgenthaler, author of the popular book *Worship Evangelism*. When she published her book in 1995, Morgenthaler was confident that the worship evangelism movement carried with it "all the conceptual and theological underpinnings necessary for longevity."[10] Eight years later, in a courageous reassessment of her work, Morgenthaler regretted that her book had given many congregations an excuse for avoiding the difficult work of outreach:

> If contemporary worship is the best witnessing tool in the box, then why give a rip about what goes on outside the worship center? If unbelievers are coming through the doors to check us Christians out, and if they'll fall at Jesus' feet after they listen to us croon worship songs and watch us sway back and forth, well, then, a whole lot of churches are just going to say, "Sign us up!"[11]

Today, Morgenthaler has taken a step back from her earlier work by stressing that worship must be more than simply "what goes on inside the tent."[12] Morgenthaler points out that although "Jesus himself spent crucial time in synagogues and the Temple" and "affirmed that worship of God is central to what it means to be a disciple," he "did not make the building — or corporate worship — the destination. His destination was the people God wanted to touch, and those were, with few exceptions, people who wouldn't have spent much time in holy places. Jesus' direction was always outward."[13] Morgenthaler cautions evangelicals, "Worship must finally become, as Paul reminds us, more life than event (Romans 12:1-2)."[14] Morganthaler's comments bring evangelical worship one step closer to realizing the title of an essay by Stanley Hauerwas: "Worship, Evangelism, Ethics: On Eliminating the 'And.'"[15] The remarks of the worship leaders interviewed above offer encouraging evidence that at Eastbrook, this synthesis is more than academic.

---

10. Saliers, "Liturgy and Ethics," p. 283.

11. Sally Morgenthaler, "Worship as Evangelism: Sally Morgenthaler Rethinks Her Own Paradigm," *Rev! Magazine* (May/June 2007): 48.

12. Morgenthaler, "Worship as Evangelism," p. 53.

13. Morgenthaler, "Worship as Evangelism," p. 53.

14. Morgenthaler, "Worship as Evangelism," p. 52.

15. Stanley M. Hauerwas, "Worship, Evangelism, Ethics: On Eliminating the 'And,'" in *Liturgy and the Moral Self,* ed. Anderson and Morrill, pp. 95-106.

Also encouraging is the fact that Eastbrook's work and worship are clearly done in cooperation, not competition, with other churches. As noted earlier, James White cautioned his colleagues that "large segments of North American Christianity have no interest in ecumenism and are doing quite well without us."[16] However, I was struck by how frequently and intentionally Eastbrook incorporated ecumenical references into its regular Sunday worship. For example, several times during my study, Marc opened the service by announcing, "Welcome to Eastbrook, and welcome especially to our visitors. If you are visiting from another church, we're glad you're here, and we ask you to please take our love back home with you. We do not want to be tearing down other churches to build up ours."

Marc told me about a conversation he had soon after his congregation purchased St. Nicholas's facility: "I went over to see the priest who was in charge of this parish, and he asked, 'Marc, why are you people so kind to us?' I said, 'Huh?' He laughed and said, 'Marc, you don't understand — we think evangelicals hate Catholics.' I replied immediately, 'Well, we love you. We're brothers and sisters in Christ, and we need to love one another.' The priest became a really good friend."

Eastbrook's ecumenical hospitality was also evident on child dedication Sunday, when Marc explained to all those assembled, "At Eastbrook, we follow a long tradition of dedicating our children and then baptizing them when they're old enough to make a commitment. This is not to cause difficulty with other churches. If you come to us from a sacramental church and you were baptized as an infant, we recognize that as a Christian baptism." Many people expressed appreciation for this sensitivity: a significant number of congregants were baptized as infants in the Roman Catholic Church. One congregant confessed that her choice to join Eastbrook was a source of some tension: "Coming out of my Catholic background . . . one of my challenges is convincing my family that my church is not anti-Catholic, but pro-Christian."

In the sermon presented at the beginning of the chapter, Marc makes clear that the body of Christ is "not a Lutheran temple, or a Protestant temple, or a nondenominational evangelical temple." Similar ecumenical references frequently pepper Marc's remarks. "Let's put ourselves in perspective: we

16. James F. White, "How Do We Know It Is Us?," in *Liturgy and the Moral Self,* ed. Anderson and Morrill, p. 58.

are only something like one five-millionth of all the churches," he reminded the congregation one Sunday. In a different service, Marc noted, "One of the things that is true for Eastbrook Church — the reason we exist, and the reason we have a future, and the reason we can be effective in the city — is because Jesus Christ is living in us. We're his body. This should be true of every church out there; Eastbrook doesn't have a corner on this." A few weeks later, Marc stressed the oneness of believers:

> In order to be a Christian, you have to be indwelt by the Spirit of God. And the Spirit indwelling a Catholic is the same Spirit indwelling a Baptist, is the same Spirit indwelling someone from Eastbrook. . . . If you put your trust in Christ, you're stuck with all the rest of us. There's nothing you can do about it. Everyone who has a genuine relationship with Christ is your brother or sister. This is the unity the Spirit gives.

Marc's words reflect Whitefield's conviction that one can regard church order as essential, or one can regard regeneration by the Holy Spirit as essential, but one cannot do both. Marc emphasized the significance of the Spirit one Sunday:

> It's amazing how there are so many churches, and we've divided into denominations, and divided into communions, and people say, "We've got to get back together!" Look: we've never stopped being together. . . . We're held together by the Holy Spirit. He's not a gas. He's not a ghost. Think of him as steel. He's eternal. He's all-powerful. And he's living in every single believer on the surface of the planet, and every single person in heaven. He's gathering a group of people, growing larger by the minute, and every one of them is indwelt by the Spirit of God. We're already united. The problem is that it's not very visible.

However, interpretation of Scripture is a key place where unity between churches is likely to break down. Ecclesiological, cultural, and personal contexts all help shape the meaning of worship; as Kevin Irwin points out, "These very *contexts* give rise to varied meanings even when the same liturgical *texts* . . . are used."[17] In recent decades, liturgical theologians have

---

17. Irwin, quoted in White, "How Do We Know It Is Us?," p. 291.

ignored a particular cultural context — the polarization of North American Protestantism into "liberal" and "conservative" theological camps — to the discipline's detriment.

In his 1988 work *The Restructuring of American Religion,* Princeton University sociologist Robert Wuthnow observed that events of the last half-century have wrought a transformation of epic proportions in American Christianity. This transformation was under way well before World War II: at the turn of the twentieth century, social events and movements in American culture — including the disagreements between Northern and Southern Christians over slavery, the rise and influence of Darwinian theory, and the influence of historical-critical study of the Bible — worked to undercut Protestant hegemony. Wuthnow emphasized that the 1960s witnessed the rise of a whole new set of issues around which "pro" or "con" positions could be taken, including the civil rights movement, the Vietnam War, and denominational mergers and schisms. Wuthnow described the post-1960s context this way: "It was as if bits of the mosaic that had given shape to the religious topography had been thrown into the air, never to land in exactly the same positions as before."[18] The period after the 1960s was one of "religious realignment," in which religious conservatives and liberals found greater commonality with fellow believers across denominational lines than with each other inside the same denomination.

Before proceeding with this discussion, I want to offer a word of caution. "Liberal" and "evangelical" are notoriously difficult words to define with precision: employing them as primary descriptors risks oversimplifying a very complex terrain. Some groups and individuals have happily adopted both terms (e.g., Jim Wallis, the founder and editor of *Sojourners* magazine, and some branches of the Mennonite Church); others do not fit easily into either classification (e.g., Southern Baptists, Nazarenes, Disciples of Christ, and Assemblies of God). Nevertheless, I retain the distinction because it has become part of the popular lexicon and because it continues to be employed at the scholarly level.

One recent example is the book *Evangelical vs. Liberal* (2008) by sociologist James K. Wellman. On the basis of an extensive study of three

---

18. Robert Wuthnow, *The Restructuring of American Religion: Society and Faith since World War II* (Princeton: Princeton University Press, 1988), p. 152.

dozen Protestant congregations, Wellman concludes that these two groups of Christians have grown increasingly divided over the nature of faith in the twenty-first century. For the purposes of his study, Wellman defines liberal Protestant churches by a distinctive set of ideological characteristics:

> They most often propose that Jesus is a model of radical inclusiveness — fashioning an ethic that emphasizes hospitality to those marginalized in society — justify themselves in their faith tradition as much by reason as by tradition or scripture, and leave decision-making about faith or personal morality in the responsible hands of the individual. The moral worldview of these churches reflects a liberal theology that advocates for the concerns and rights of homosexuals; and supports justice causes such as peace, ending homelessness, and ecological stewardship.[19]

Conversely, evangelical churches are generally those who

> emphasize conversion (the need for a personal decision to follow Jesus Christ), missionary activity (the obligation to share with others this need for conversion), Biblicism (seeing the Scriptures as the sole authority for belief and action), and crucicentrism (the belief in Christ's sacrifice on the cross as atonement for human sin).[20]

Wellman reports a remarkable depth of disagreement between the two groups on multiple fronts, a few of which will be explored below.

Liberals and evangelicals have developed quite different strategies for reconciling their accounts of divine action with a scientific worldview. Evangelicals have adopted an interventionist approach to divine action, wherein "God is sovereign over the laws of nature and is able to overrule them to produce special divine acts."[21] Theologian Millard Erickson is representative of the interventionist position: he defines miracles as "those special super-

19. James K. Wellman, *Evangelical vs. Liberal: The Clash of Christian Cultures in the Pacific Northwest* (New York: Oxford University Press, 2008), p. 5.

20. Wellman, *Evangelical vs. Liberal,* p. 11.

21. Nancey Murphy, *Beyond Liberalism and Fundamentalism: How Modern and Post-Modern Philosophy Set the Theological Agenda* (London and New York: Continuum/Trinity Press International, 1996), p. 63.

natural works of God's providence which are not explicable on the basis of the usual patterns of nature."[22]

For their part, many liberal Christians have adopted an immanentist approach that emphasizes God's action in and through all natural processes. According to this view, an "act of God" is not a particular act performed from time to time in history and nature, but rather "the 'master act' in which God is involved, namely the whole course of history."[23] Gordon Kaufman's work is representative of the immanentist position. According to him, "There is no God who 'walks and talks with me' in close interpersonal communion, giving his full attention to my complaints, miraculously extracting me from difficulties into which I have gotten myself by invading nature and history with *ad hoc* rescue operations from on high."[24] Kaufman explains that God does not work by "violently ripping into the fabric of history or arbitrarily upsetting the momentum of its powers."[25] Instead, God's power is manifest "within and through the closely textured and natural historical processes of our modern experience."[26] Thus, for Kaufman, the paradigm of divine action is "the story of a man praying that this cup might pass from him, that prayer not answered with legions of angels to rescue him but with lonely suffering on the cross; but this is followed by the birth of faith and hope in a new community after his death."[27]

In his study of liberal and evangelical congregations in the Pacific Northwest, Wellman noted a similar phenomenon: "I was struck by the caution among liberals to discuss how they related to God in personal terms. . . . One did not hear, as in conversation with evangelicals, about what the 'Lord was doing in my life,' or how 'God had healed me,' or what 'God was teaching me.' "[28] What became clear to Wellman was that liberals "did not ask God for this or that thing in particular; God is not expected to intervene in the

22. Millard Erickson, *Christian Theology,* one-volume edition (Grand Rapids: Baker, 1983), p. 406.

23. Murphy, *Beyond Liberalism and Fundamentalism,* p. 73.

24. Gordon Kaufman, "On the Meaning of 'Act of God,'" *Harvard Theological Review* 61 (1968): 156.

25. Kaufman, "On the Meaning of 'Act of God,'" p. 157.

26. Kaufman, in Murphy, *Beyond Liberalism and Fundamentalism,* p. 63.

27. Kaufman, in Murphy, *Beyond Liberalism and Fundamentalism,* p. 73.

28. Wellman, *Evangelical vs. Liberal,* pp. 140-41.

details of one's life." If God did do something, it was to be "present" in the world — and Wellman stresses that this sense of "presence" is by no means superficial, but rather "a powerful instrument of grace, love, and acceptance for liberals."[29] In Nancey Murphy's assessment, it would be difficult to overstate the differences between the interventionist and immanentist positions:

> There may be no other single factor that has such thoroughgoing consequences for theology; thus, the divide between liberals and conservatives on this issue opens a veritable chasm between their theological outlooks. . . . This issue is of fundamental importance in determining theologians' views on theological method and Scripture: immanentism requires an experiential foundation for theology, since Scriptural foundationalism is dependent upon an interventionist view of revelation. One's view of revelation in turn affects one's theory of religious language and the positions available regarding the relationship between science and religion.[30]

One of the most salient differences between evangelicals and liberals is their contrasting approaches to Scripture. In his book with Peggy Shriver called *The Divided Church*, Richard Hutcheson Jr. identifies a difference between the liberal approach and the evangelical approach to historical criticism: liberals tend to "approach the task from the scientific side — criticism is a given, and the liberal looks for the religious values still to be found in the Bible despite its human and historical conditioning."[31] Conversely, evangelicals approach "from the biblical side — the authority of Scripture is a given, and the question is how criticism can help to understand it."[32]

For evangelicals, "the scriptures are dangerous precisely because they confront sin and refuse rationalization of sin."[33] For liberals, the Bible is dangerous in a different way: "it can be used to exclude and condemn the very people liberals include — gay people and others who are socially vul-

29. Wellman, *Evangelical vs. Liberal,* p. 141.

30. Murphy, *Beyond Liberalism and Fundamentalism,* p. 63.

31. Richard G. Hutcheson Jr. and Peggy Shriver, *The Divided Church: Moving Liberals and Conservatives from Diatribe to Dialogue* (Downers Grove, Ill.: InterVarsity Press, 1999), p. 33.

32. Hutcheson Jr. and Shriver, *The Divided Church,* p. 33.

33. Wellman, *Evangelical vs. Liberal,* p. 108.

nerable."[34] Relatedly, Wellman observed differences between the two groups' soteriologies: "Whereas the cross for liberals is a symbol that confronts social injustice and human self-righteousness, for evangelicals the cross is a battle for the human soul between God and Satan."[35]

I cite these studies to suggest that liberal-evangelical theological differences are more divisive for unity than current liturgical scholarship acknowledges. Twentieth-century liturgical scholars stressed liturgy as an event with a *shape*. Anton Baumstark proposed that structures of worship were the surest ground for comparing different liturgical traditions, Gregory Dix rooted the "shape of the liturgy" in New Testament texts, and Alexander Schmemann sought to find the core structure that holds together the church's liturgical life.[36] Today, many scholars recommend liturgical shape as a fruitful starting point for ecumenical dialogue:

> It is no longer sufficient to discuss the meaning of "Roman Catholic ritual" or "Lutheran liturgy" . . . the similarity — in the patterns and in the problems, in the full Christian heritage and in the current human horizon — of all the actual local gatherings for worship makes possible an ecumenical liturgical theology.[37]

In this spirit of optimism, Eugene Brand rejoices that "separatedness because of classic dogmatic differences in the understanding of the sacraments and the ordained ministry is being challenged by the pragmatic impact of the celebrated liturgy."[38] Liturgical scholars share Brand's hope that "remaining differences in doctrine and polity will be resolved — or forgotten" as "worship in common [forges] relationships which, in the end, will prove irresistible."[39]

A common liturgical *ordo* might indeed help magisterial churches overcome denominational differences in sacramental theology, polity, and ordi-

34. Wellman, *Evangelical vs. Liberal*, p. 108.

35. Wellman, *Evangelical vs. Liberal*, p. 267.

36. Gordon W. Lathrop, *Holy Things: A Liturgical Theology* (Minneapolis: Fortress Press, 1993), p. 33.

37. Lathrop, *Holy Things*, p. 44.

38. Eugene Brand, "Berakah Response: Ecumenism and the Liturgy," *Worship* 58 (1984): 307-8.

39. Brand, "Berakah Response," pp. 307-8.

nation. However, my congregational studies indicate that these are not the most pressing of all theological issues for many Free Church congregations. For example, Marc explained his approach to the Lord's Supper to me this way: "I don't get up and argue about transubstantiation or consubstantiation or spiritual presence, or any of those things. We just assume that God is with us and having table fellowship with us. If Roman Catholics come here and believe in transubstantiation, I don't correct them. This makes people uncomfortable. They would like me to be Zwingli, or Calvin, or Luther, or Council of Trent. Those theological distinctions aren't so important to me. What I do emphasize at the Lord's Supper is that *we* are the body of Christ."

A far more significant theological issue for Marc surfaced in his account of an Easter service celebrated jointly by Eastbrook and several churches from a different section of the city. Marc expressed dismay over the fact that, from his perspective, the service "was all about freedom, liberation from evil, the power of new life," but "nothing was said about the historical resurrection of Jesus." "Needless to say, that [ecumenical effort] didn't end well," he sighed.

Marc's comments suggest that there are at least *two* sets of ecumenical obstacles that liturgical theologians working in a North American context must address. On the one hand are the "classic dogmatic differences" Brand references above — those sacramental and theological disputes at the heart of the churches' divisions in the sixteenth century. These are the issues that receive the majority of scholarly attention in liturgical studies. However, the Fundamentalist-Modernist controversies of the early twentieth century have created new dogmatic debates in North America concerning the historicity of Scripture, the authority of science, and the nature of God's action in the world. North American evangelical churches are largely "products of controversies within mainline denominations that have gone liberal";[40] therefore, for many evangelicals in the pews, these early-twentieth-century controversies are of much greater importance than the sacramental debates of the sixteenth century.

The tension between these "scholarly level" and "pew level" ecumenical priorities clearly emerges by comparing two documents. The first, a Faith and Order Paper by the World Council of Churches entitled "Toward Koinonia in Worship," suggests that "the patterns of word and table, of catechetical

---

40. Simon Chan, *Liturgical Theology* (Downers Grove, Ill.: IVP Academic, 2006), p. 15.

formation and baptism, of Sunday and the week, of *Pascha* and the year, and of assembly and ministry around these things" offer the churches the basis for a mutually encouraging conversation. Churches may "call each other toward a maturation in the use of this pattern or a renewed clarification of its central characteristics or, even, toward a conversion to its use."[41] However, a second example, written by an evangelical author and directed to a popular audience, indicates that ecumenical conversations will need to include more than discussions of liturgical shape:

> I also would say that a church's use of a liturgical approach does not mean that the church will produce healthy disciples. . . . One can go through the motions of liturgy as many very liberal churches do, saying the same words with their rich theology. Yet their lives do not reflect what I consider that of a healthy disciple if they do not hold to the inspired and authoritative Scriptures and other key doctrines regarding who God is and reflect those in their lives. . . . In fact, to my understanding the more extreme liberal churches and the ones that I personally feel have strayed from the purity of the gospel are ones that generally use liturgical worship.[42]

Many conservative evangelical churches would be quick to point out that while it may be true that worshippers across a variety of confessional traditions now "wear similar vesture, arrange the church furniture in similar ways, share the same lectionary, sing the same hymns, adopt the same basic outline or shape of the liturgy, and even use many of the same liturgical texts,"[43] it is emphatically *not* true that these congregations interpret Scripture or understand the nature of God's action in the world in the same ways. To cite but one possible example, it makes a significant difference whether the congregation celebrating the liturgy understands the first eleven chapters of Genesis to be stories of origin or historical reports, and whether

---

41. See Gordon W. Lathrop, *Holy People: A Liturgical Ecclesiology* (Minneapolis: Fortress Press, 1999), p. 231.

42. Dan Kimball, "Responses to Timothy C. J. Quill, 'Liturgical Position,'" in *Perspectives on Christian Worship: Five Views*, ed. J. Matthew Pinson (Nashville: Broadman & Holman, 2009), p. 97.

43. Paul F. Bradshaw, "The Homogenization of Christian Liturgy — Ancient and Modern," *Studia Liturgica* 26 (1996): 10.

it interprets the virgin birth, Jesus' miracles, and the Resurrection as literal fact or broken myth. This is why, for churches like Eastbrook, it is less the practice of a particular liturgical "shape" and more the theological content of the prayers, songs, and sermons offered *within* that shape that determines whether worship is faithful to the Christian tradition. These critical ecumenical conversations about Scripture and liturgical structure will be taken up in the next two chapters.

CHAPTER THREE

Fundamentalism versus Rite?
Rethinking the Scripture/Liturgy Relationship

[Evangelical Christianity] is able to sustain meaningful belief in God by encapsulating itself in a sort of pre-modern cocoon. God is seen as intervening directly in human affairs; prayers are, or can be, answered miraculously; there is a strong sense of demarcation between the believing community and its unbelieving environment; the words of the Bible are regarded as qualitatively different from all other human utterances. It is just conceivable that, in an age of secularity, the only way of making sense of belief is to draw a kind of line around it, to mark it off, and to espouse some such pre-modern view of reality. . . . But there is a limit to this capacity. Incredulity awaits.

Graham Hughes, *Worship as Meaning*

[Paul] Ricoeur talks about a second naïveté. Naïveté on the prior side of grappling with complexity isn't worth much, but a second naïveté on the other side of grappling is worth a great deal. And evangelicals, of the sophisticated sort, believe that's where we are. Overgeneralizations that try to paint us as being obscurantist and outmoded just don't work. They simply aren't true.

Pastor Phil Thorne, West Shore Evangelical Free Church

The fact that different parts of the church read Scripture in profoundly differ-ent ways compounds the difficulty of writing an ecumenical liturgical the-ology. On the one hand, the Bible itself is a symbol of unity. The ecumenical movement began with the basic assumption that despite all its bitter divi-sions, the church is drawn together by Holy Scripture, which constitutes the supreme authority of Christian faith and life. Emilio Castro, former general secretary of the World Council of Churches, stresses that "the Bible is God's authoritative word for both the ecumenical movement and evangelicals" and urges both groups to read the Bible together.[1] Ironically, however, biblical interpretation is one of the most divisive subjects within ecumenism. For example, George Lindbeck worries that Castro's proposal seems "impossi-bly visionary," given the fact that the circles in which popular, serious Bible reading is most widespread are "often fundamentalist and almost always precritical in their hermeneutics."[2]

David Kelsey's groundbreaking work *The Uses of Scripture in Recent Theology* (1975) provides a fruitful contextual starting point. Kelsey observes that even before theologians begin to use Scripture to prove doctrine, they must make a prior judgment about how the Bible functions authoritatively. In Kelsey's account, fundamentalists and evangelicals believe that Scripture is authoritative because it contains revealed propositions. Kelsey cites the work of the late-nineteenth-century theologian B. B. Warfield as representative of this position. According to Warfield,

> "The Bible is inspired not *in part* but *fully*, in all its elements alike — things discoverable by reason as well as mysteries, matters of history and science as well as of faith and practice, words as well as thoughts." So understood, [says Kelsey,] the Bible is not simply a record of revelation; it is rather revelation itself. It is the very Word of God itself, a Word of God in which God speaks directly to each of our souls.[3]

---

1. Emilio Castro, "Ecumenism and Evangelicalism: Where Are We?," in *Faith and Faith-fulness: Essays on Contemporary Ecumenical Themes — A Tribute to Phillip A. Potter* (Geneva: World Council of Churches, 1984), p. 15.

2. George A. Lindbeck, "Two Kinds of Ecumenism: Unitive and Interdenominational," *Gregorianum* 70, no. 4 (1989): 659.

3. See David H. Kelsey, *The Uses of Scripture in Recent Theology* (Philadelphia: Fortress Press, 1975), p. 17.

Since the authoritative aspect of Scripture is the inspired doctrine that it teaches, Warfield understands the task of theology to be defining biblical doctrines and systematically interrelating them.

Ten years later, George Lindbeck turned Warfield's biblical theology into a "cognitive propositionalist" theory of doctrine.[4] According to Lindbeck, cognitive propositionalists believe that doctrines are analogous to scientific propositions: they function as truth claims about objective realities. If a doctrine is once true, it is always true, and if it is once false, it is always false. This, Lindbeck notes, is a decidedly unhelpful approach to ecumenical dialogue: it creates a situation in which there can only be winners and losers.

Throughout their work, both Kelsey and Lindbeck critique the perceived inflexibility of the evangelical position. Kelsey notes that Warfield's construal of Scripture as a holy object in and through which Christians experience numinous power is no longer seriously imaginable for many American Christians: "to insist that a Christian community now adopt [Warfield's] hypothesis might seem a demand that it archaize itself into a culture now gone, much as though it were being required to adopt a pre-Copernican man's attitudes toward the heavens."[5] Lindbeck concurs, suggesting that cognitive propositionalists have a tendency to "combine unusual insecurity with naïveté."[6] More recently, liturgical scholar Graham Hughes has warned of an inherent "conceptual brittleness": although evangelicalism offers adherents "a clarity, a simplicity, an accessibility not obviously afforded in pluralistic societies," Hughes is unconvinced that these short-term successes bespeak the movement's long-term viability.[7]

But charges of naïveté, conceptual brittleness, and archaism have perpetuated a false dichotomy: liturgical churches that embrace higher biblical criticism on one side, and hermeneutically immature fundamentalist churches on the other. Over the last thirty years, evangelicals have grown in hermeneutical sophistication. Alister McGrath and David Wenham now commend evangelicals for "welcoming the critical method in principle, yet denying that its implementation necessarily undermines, in theory or practice, the

---

4. George A. Lindbeck, *The Nature of Doctrine: Religion and Theology in a Postliberal Age* (London: SPCK, 1984), p. 16.

5. Kelsey, *The Uses of Scripture in Recent Theology*, p. 172.

6. Lindbeck, *The Nature of Doctrine*, p. 21.

7. Graham Hughes, *Worship as Meaning: A Liturgical Theology for Late Modernity* (Cambridge: Cambridge University Press, 2003), p. 242.

historic Christian conviction concerning the divine authority of Scripture."[8] In his book *Between Faith and Criticism: Evangelicals, Scholarship, and the Bible in America,* historian Mark Noll similarly praises the rise of "believing criticism" in evangelical scholarship, which he defines as "the creative confluence of confidence in Scripture as the Word of God and dedication to the solid results of research wherever they are found."[9]

What do recent developments in biblical studies mean for the Scripture/liturgy relationship in evangelical and ecumenical thought? The first half of this chapter puts the answers given by Roman Catholic liturgical scholars Aidan Kavanagh and Louis-Marie Chauvet in conversation with evangelical systematic theologian John Webster. The second half of the chapter places the biblical-liturgical work of Lutheran liturgical scholar Gordon Lathrop in conversation with the work of evangelical systematician Kevin Vanhoozer. All parties surveyed share the same concern: fundamentalism is an inappropriate divinization of Scripture. However, the liturgical correctives offered by Kavanagh, Chauvet, and Lathrop differ from the theological proposals of Webster and Vanhoozer on a number of key theological points. As we will see, evangelicals make their own distinctive ecumenical contribution to the problem of fundamentalism by emphasizing the Trinitarian nature of revelation and the diversity of biblical genres.

Aidan Kavanagh

According to liturgical scholar Aidan Kavanagh, the problem of biblical fundamentalism began with the invention of the printing press. Prior to Gutenberg, humanity encountered God through burning bushes, holy symbols, and church windows, as well as through "ambiguous actions done with oil, food, and the touch of human hands."[10] Furthermore, ordinary Jews

8. Alister McGrath and David Wenham, "Evangelicalism and Biblical Authority," in *Evangelical Anglicans: Their Role and Influence in the Church Today,* ed. R. T. France and A. E. McGrath (London: SPCK, 1993), p. 31.

9. Mark A. Noll, *Between Faith and Criticism: Evangelicals, Scholarship, and the Bible in America* (San Francisco: Harper & Row, 1986), p. 164.

10. Aidan Kavanagh, *On Liturgical Theology* (Yonkers, N.Y.: Pueblo Publishing Co., 1992), p. 108.

and Christians experienced Scripture as an *oral* event that regularly took place in the context of public worship. Scripture and liturgy were "less two different enterprises than a single effort carried out in distinct but deeply related modes by a group of people sharing a common trust in the validity of what they were doing."[11]

The situation declined rapidly in the sixteenth century as the new technology of the printing press, working in tandem with the Protestant principle of *sola scriptura,* domesticated God into mere text, proposition, and doctrine. Although it would be too much to say that printing reduced God's Word into words (writing itself was responsible for that), Kavanagh suggests "it would be true to say that printing turned God's Words into a text which all people, literate or not, could now see as lines of type marching across a page."[12] He continues:

> God's Word could now for the first time be visualized by all, not in the multivalency of a "presence" in corporate act or icon, but linearly in horizontal lines which could be edited, reset, revised, fragmented, and studied by all — something which few could have done before. A Presence which had formerly been experienced by most as a kind of enfolding embrace had now modulated into an abecedarian printout to which only the skill of literacy could give complete access.[13]

Kavanagh protests this development: "The Judeo-Christian tradition accords the written Scriptures marks of deepest veneration, [but] it has never regarded the written Scriptures, whether in Torah scrolls or in gospel book, as the object of the liturgical cult."[14] In short, biblical fundamentalism is nothing less than idolatry.

For Kavanagh, the corrective lies in re-establishing the logical priority of liturgy over Scripture. The early church did not wait for the full development and canonization of Christian Scripture before beginning its practice of liturgical worship. Instead, "the written texts of the Christian bible, as

11. Aidan Kavanagh, "Scripture and Worship in Synagogue and Church," *Michigan Quarterly Review* 22 (1983): 492.

12. Kavanagh, *On Liturgical Theology,* p. 104.

13. Kavanagh, *On Liturgical Theology,* p. 104.

14. Kavanagh, "Scripture and Worship in Synagogue and Church," p. 480.

they emerged, entered into worship patterns that were already established —
especially in the synagogal, paschal, and domestic usages of Judaism which
the earliest Christians continued to employ even as they began to fill them
with a new content."[15] Put differently, Christian scriptures were conceived
within the liturgical womb of Judaism as evangelists, apostolic writers, and
others gave new content to Jewish hymns, prayers, and worship structures.[16]

Because Scripture and liturgy are two sides of the same coin, Kavanagh
argues that the best solution to the problem of fundamentalism is to reunite
them under the heading of *rite*. In the Incarnation, "God welds himself to us,
and us to himself, without confusion." In liturgy too, "God welds himself into
our media of discourse without becoming subordinate either to those media
or to us who must use them."[17] Today, this coterminous understanding of
Scripture and liturgy must be recovered. The former is the oral and written
account of the assembly's historic faith experience; the latter is the enactment
of that same experience in a complementary medium.[18]

There is much in Kavanagh's account with which evangelicals can agree.
For instance, systematic theologian John Webster applauds Kavanagh's insistence that Christian worship is "worship of the Utterer of the divine Word,
but it is not worship of written Scripture."[19] Webster similarly emphasizes,
"At his glorification to the Father's right hand, Jesus does not resign his office
of self-communication, handing it over to the texts of Scripture which are
henceforth in and of themselves his voice in the world."[20] Like Kavanagh,
Webster believes that biblical fundamentalism "runs the risk of attributing to
the text perfections which are properly attributed to God alone." No divine
nature or properties are to be predicated of Scripture: "its substance is that
of a creaturely reality (even if it is a creaturely reality annexed to the self-
presentation of God); and its relation to God is instrumental."[21]

---

15. Aidan Kavanagh, *The Shape of Baptism: The Rite of Christian Initiation* (Yonkers, N.Y.:
Pueblo Publishing Co., 1978), p. xiii.

16. Kavanagh, *On Liturgical Theology*, p. 111.

17. Kavanagh, *On Liturgical Theology*, p. 120.

18. See Kavanagh, "Scripture and Worship in Synagogue and Church," p. 485.

19. Kavanagh, "Scripture and Worship in Synagogue and Church," p. 480.

20. John Webster, *Holy Scripture: A Dogmatic Sketch* (Cambridge: Cambridge University
Press, 2003), p. 189.

21. Webster, *Holy Scripture*, p. 22.

Despite these points of agreement, Webster offers three correctives to Kavanagh's liturgical/biblical proposal. First, Webster worries that Kavanagh's historical assertions — that is, "Neither Scripture nor liturgy write or enact themselves; they are things which a group of people who share common patterns of belief do when they come together to worship God," and "Scripture and liturgical worship are correlative functions of that fundamental entity, the human assembly"[22] — are pneumatologically thin. Webster points out that "the phenomena of church life — words, rites, order, history, and the rest — do not automatically, as it were *ex opere operato,* constitute the communion of saints; rather, the church becomes what it is as the Spirit animates the forms so that they indicate the presence of God."[23] Put differently, the Spirit is not promised and given "in a way which is convertible into something immanent to the church, which the church realizes in its action. Rather, the Spirit is other than the church, the one for whose coming the church must pray: *Veni, creator Spiritus.*"[24]

Second, Webster is troubled by Kavanagh's analogy between liturgy and the Incarnation. Kavanagh writes,

> In the liturgy, God welds himself into the media of our discourse without becoming subordinate either to those media or to us who must use them. . . . God does not merely *use* a human medium such as a human nature, a writing, or a liturgical event to disclose himself as it were from afar. Rather, God welds himself into the human medium while never becoming subordinate to it.[25]

However, Webster insists that "incarnation" cannot be extended into a general theological principle of divine action without threatening the uniqueness of the Word's becoming flesh. Instead, Webster proposes thinking of Scripture as a "sanctified" text. Because the texts of Scripture are creaturely, "all the tools of its creatureliness are legitimate: grammar, source criticism,

---

22. Kavanagh, "Scripture and Worship in Synagogue and Church," p. 485; and Kavanagh, *On Liturgical Theology,* p. 111.

23. John Webster, *Confessing God: Essay in Christian Dogmatics II* (London: T&T Clark, 2005), p. 181.

24. Webster, *Confessing God,* p. 183.

25. Kavanagh, *On Liturgical Theology,* p. 120.

redaction criticism, and so forth." At the same time, for Webster biblical texts are not to be defined and handled *exclusively* as creaturely entities: they are also "fields of the Spirit's action in the publication of the knowledge of God."[26]

This emphasis on the Holy Spirit leads to a third critique: the problem of fundamentalism is not that Scripture has been severed from its liturgical context, but that it has been severed from its *Trinitarian* context. Paraphrasing Barth, Kevin Vanhoozer explains that the Triune God is "the communicator, the communication, and the 'communicatedness' of Scripture."[27] As Father, God is the origin of revelation — "the utterer, the begetter, [and] the sustainer of words," the one who formerly spoke through the prophets and now speaks through the Son (Heb. 1:1-2).[28] As Son, God actualizes his self-presence in revelation. Jesus Christ is the content of the Father's message: "risen from the dead, he is the living Word who declares with authority the full effect, the reality of, and benefits which flow from his reconciling achievement."[29] As Spirit, God reveals the perfection of his self-revelation by making it real and effective in the history of humankind.[30] This leads to Webster's concern. Fundamentalism results when the inspired product is given priority over the revelatory, sanctifying, and inspiring activities of the Triune God:

> [Scripture] becomes reified into an independent entity whose nature and operations can be grasped apart from the network of relations in which it is properly located. And like other historical realities within that economy — temple, cult, kingship, sacraments, order — reification means distortion, for like those other realities, Scripture has its being in reference to the activity of God. If that reference is damaged or distorted, its true character is obscured.[31]

26. Webster, *Confessing God*, p. 48.

27. Quoted in Kevin J. Vanhoozer, *The Drama of Doctrine: A Canonical-Linguistic Approach to Christian Theology* (Louisville: Westminster John Knox Press, 2005), p. 67.

28. Kevin Vanhoozer, "God's Mighty Speech-Acts: The Doctrine of Scripture Today," in *A Pathway into the Holy Scripture,* ed. Philip E. Satterthwaite and David F. Wright (Grand Rapids: Wm. B. Eerdmans, 1994), p. 177.

29. Webster, *Confessing God*, p. 49.

30. See Webster, *Holy Scripture*, p. 14.

31. John Webster, *Word and Church: Essays in Christian Dogmatics* (Edinburgh: T&T Clark, 2001), p. 28.

On a historical level, Kavanagh is correct in emphasizing liturgical worship as the *Sitz im Leben* of canonical Scripture. However, Webster makes clear that on a theological level, "Scripture is [not] the church's invention, whether through production or authorization, and still less because the church is Scripture's patron, conferring some dignity on it by adopting it as its symbol system of choice."[32] When liturgical scholars argue that "the liturgical assembly is the place where the Bible becomes the Bible" and that "the book is nothing without the community," Webster counters that the church's authorization and commendation of the canon have "noetic but not ontological force" — the church *acknowledges* what Scripture is but does not *make* it so.[33]

Louis-Marie Chauvet

A second understanding of the Scripture/liturgy relationship in Catholic thought comes from liturgical scholar Louis-Marie Chauvet. Throughout his work, Chauvet is concerned with refuting a metaphysical literary understanding wherein authors deposit meanings in texts, which readers then attempt to decode and reproduce. This classic hermeneutic presupposes that universal truth transcends local contingencies — indeed, that the language and sociocultural situations of the author and readers are merely "coverings" for the translation of truth. As a result, the reader's failure to master the author's meaning is "due to a simple accident, as unfortunate as it is inevitable."[34]

By contrast, Chauvet embraces a postmodern semiolinguistic theory of texts that casts the difference between authors and readers in a very different light. Chauvet draws on the work of Roland Barthes to explain that every piece of writing is followed by a moment of retreat: the writer disappears from his or her product and leaves it behind as a testament. In Chauvet's words, "the author dies in her or his work in order to affirm through it her or his victory over death."[35] Such is the fate of writing: it is capable of coming

32. Webster, *Confessing God*, p. 53.

33. Louis-Marie Chauvet, *Symbol and Sacrament: A Sacramental Reinterpretation of Christian Existence* (Collegeville, Minn.: Liturgical Press, 1995), pp. 212, 209; and Webster, *Word and Church*, p. 39.

34. Chauvet, *Symbol and Sacrament*, pp. 204-5.

35. Chauvet, *Symbol and Sacrament*, p. 206.

into being only by becoming other than its author. This is especially true when it comes to "the *myths* and the *books held sacred* by various reading groups": an invented story can become a myth only "when it loses its author and so becomes the collective coded expression of the identity of the group which 'believes it.'"[36]

According to Chauvet, all texts are written and read from within socially arranged and culturally constructed worlds — there is no "neutral place that sovereignly transcends all socio-historical determinations."[37] Furthermore, reading is more than the simple act of decoding an author's meaning: it is "the symbolic act of producing a *new text,* and original word, on the basis of the rules of the game decoded from the text."[38] Put differently, upon the "death" of the author, the book is given over to readers, who become its "operators." Following Mallarmé, Chauvet stresses that "the very being of a book depends on its history and the multiple readings of which it is the object."[39] In this way, reading engages the reader and his or her world as subject, causing "the same text to inspire different interpretations in different readers."[40] This means that the difference between the intention of an author and acts of interpretation by readers is not an obstacle to be overcome, but an "otherness" to be assumed, appreciated, and celebrated.[41] Chauvet concludes that believing communities who find their identity in the Bible are obligated to carry out this approach. In his summary, he notes, "Neither from the text alone, nor from the reader alone, but from the always unpredictable encounter between the two does biblical truth — a symbolic truth — arise."[42]

Although Chauvet is comfortable applying postmodern literary hermeneutics to the reading of Scripture, theologian John Webster is decidedly not. First, Webster argues that generic literary theories of texts have scant theological utility for scriptural texts: they are "developed in relative isolation from theological considerations, and in such a way as to neutralize, absorb, or sometimes even repudiate theological talk of the place of the biblical

36. Chauvet, *Symbol and Sacrament,* p. 208.
37. Chauvet, *Symbol and Sacrament,* p. 205.
38. Chauvet, *Symbol and Sacrament,* p. 205.
39. Chauvet, *Symbol and Sacrament,* p. 206.
40. Chauvet, *Symbol and Sacrament,* p. 205.
41. Chauvet, *Symbol and Sacrament,* p. 205.
42. Chauvet, *Symbol and Sacrament,* p. 209.

texts in the revelatory activity of God."[43] While Webster does not deny that "Scripture (the human text which God sanctifies for the service of his communicative presence) is still 'Scripture' (human writing generated and used by religious communities)," he is adamant that theologians not allow the specificity of the former to be folded into the generality of the latter.[44] As a corrective, Webster asserts that Scripture's being is defined "not simply by its membership in the class of text, but by the fact that it is *this* text — sanctified, that is, Spirit-generated and preserved — in *this* field of action — the communicative economy of God's merciful friendship with his lost creatures."[45]

In particular, Webster finds postmodern hermeneutical theology "decidedly attenuated" by its tendency to "take its bearings from accounts of Christian selfhood borrowed from outside Christian theology."[46] According to Webster, a dogmatic account of the reading of Scripture is inseparable from a Christian theological anthropology. Theologians must pay greater attention to what it means to read scriptural texts as *reconciled sinners*.[47] Recall that in classic hermeneutical theory, the distance between an author's meaning and the reader's interpretation was an obstacle to be overcome. For Chauvet, the irreducible socio-historical otherness of the biblical text is to be embraced: God's revelation "resists every attempt at an 'idealist' reduction of the letter that would, by appealing to a 'spiritual' sense understood as timeless truth, erase the historical contingency under the pretext of better revealing the 'Word of God.'"[48] Web-

43. Webster, *Confessing God*, p. 35.

44. Webster, *Holy Scripture*, p. 2.

45. Webster, *Holy Scripture*, p. 29.

46. Webster, *Holy Scripture*, p. 92.

47. John Webster, "Reading Scripture Eschatologically (I)," in *Reading Texts, Seeking Wisdom: Scripture and Theology*, ed. David F. Ford and Graham Stanton (Grand Rapids: Wm. B. Eerdmans, 2003), p. 247.

48. Chauvet, *Symbol and Sacrament*, p. 215. Chauvet emphasizes that "the sacramentality of this Writing goes together with respect for the letter as letter, that is, with respect for its *concrete social and cultural delimitations*. Each time, it is singular historical destinies that mediate God's revelation: this person (Abraham), this people (Israel), this particular Jew (Jesus)." See also Louis-Marie Chauvet, *The Sacraments: The Word of God at the Mercy of the Body* (Collegeville, Minn.: Liturgical Press, 2001), 46ff.: "As can be seen, the sacramentality of the Scriptures prohibits any fundamentalist reading. Indeed, the letter is here, absolutely impossible to bypass since it is, irreplaceably, the original source. . . . The Spirit is not found in spite of the letter but through it."

ster finds both proposals lacking. We do not read well, he points out, "not only because of technical incompetence, cultural distance from the substance of the text, or lack of readerly sophistication, but also and most of all because in reading Scripture we are addressed by that which runs clean counter to our will."[49]

Because human beings are unavoidably prone to fashioning Scripture into "something which pleases rather than something which disturbs or judges or commands or calls to repentance," Webster argues that Christian reading is not within the range of human competence.[50] Indeed, this is precisely why Webster is uncomfortable with postmodern assertions of reading as a symbolic act of producing a new text on the basis of the rules of the game decoded from the text. "Christian theology," Webster insists, "will surely be troubled by any account of the reader's intentions which gives such significance to reading decisions that reading the text in effect becomes rewriting it."[51] Our "perverse desire to hold the text in thrall and to employ it as an extension of our will" needs to be slain, and this "can only be achieved through an act which is not our own."[52]

As a corrective, Webster explains that "reading Scripture is an episode in the history of sin and its overcoming; and overcoming sin is the sole work of Christ and the Spirit."[53] This means that reading Scripture is inescapably bound to regeneration: the reader's will "needs not simply to be called to redirect itself to appropriate ends, but to be reborn."[54] Properly ordered reading is characterized by "a certain passivity, a respect for and receptivity towards the text, a readiness to be addressed and confronted": in short, a true reading of Scripture can occur only as a kind of brokenness.[55] At the same time, Webster stresses that faithful reading must be simultaneously characterized by restoration and reconstitution:

> To stop short of this point would be to risk denying that sin has been indeed set aside. One of the functions of a genuinely operative pneuma-

49. Webster, *Holy Scripture*, p. 87.
50. Webster, *Word and Church*, p. 79.
51. Webster, *Word and Church*, p. 81.
52. Webster, "Reading Scripture Eschatologically (I)," p. 254.
53. Webster, "Reading Scripture Eschatologically (I)," p. 254.
54. Webster, "Reading Scripture Eschatologically (I)," p. 254.
55. Webster, *Word and Church*, p. 80; see also Webster, *Holy Scripture*, p. 88.

tology in this context is to articulate grounds for the reader's *confidence* that it is possible to read Scripture well — having in mind the true ends of Scripture, with false desire and distraction held in check, and with reason and spirit quickened into alertness to the speeches of God.[56]

This confidence is wholly dependent upon the Holy Spirit, who illuminates the reader so that "exegetical reason may trust the promise of Christ to lead into truth by the Spirit's presence and power."[57]

In contrast to Chauvet's assertion that the Bible reaches its truth as the word of God when it is "raised from its death" by the living voices of the reader and homilist,[58] Webster counters that it is *Scripture* that brings about the *reader's* mortification and vivification. Drawing on a baptismal theological anthropology, Webster urges Christians to "envisage the act of reading Scripture as an instance of the fundamental pattern of all Christian existence, which is dying and rising with Jesus Christ through the purging and quickening power of the Holy Spirit."[59] Biblical truth does not arise from the "unpredictable encounter"[60] between the text and the reader because Scripture is not "an initial stage of a process of divine communication which is only fully realized in the life of the church." Instead, "Scripture bears witness to divine revelation in its perfection."[61]

Kavanagh, Chauvet, and Webster agree on the diagnosis of a common problem: evangelicals, particularly at the popular level, tend to have a "'dropped out of the sky' understanding of the Bible" that comes dangerously close to textual deification.[62] Against this understanding, Kavanagh emphasizes that although the Christian tradition accords the written Scriptures marks of the deepest veneration, it has never regarded them as the object of the liturgical cult. That role has always been reserved for God alone.[63]

---

56. Webster, *Holy Scripture*, p. 91.
57. Webster, *Holy Scripture*, p. 91.
58. Chauvet, *The Sacraments*, p. 47.
59. Webster, *Holy Scripture*, pp. 87-88.
60. Chauvet, *Symbol and Sacrament*, p. 209.
61. Webster, *Confessing God*, pp. 189-90.
62. Craig D. Allert, *A High View of Scripture? The Authority of the Bible and the Formation of the New Testament Canon* (Grand Rapids: Baker Academic, 2007), pp. 10, 12.
63. Kavanagh, "Scripture and Worship," p. 480.

Chauvet raises a similar concern: "The principle 'Christ-in-the-Scriptures' can be put forward in so unilateral and exclusive a manner that one no longer respects the symbolic otherness of the Risen One."[64]

For Chauvet and Kavanagh, the solution to fundamentalism is to return Scripture to its rightful liturgical context. As noted above, Kavanagh stresses that Christian scriptures were conceived within the liturgical womb of Judaism.[65] In a similar vein, Chauvet observes that Christian Eucharistic and baptismal assemblies "seem to have functioned empirically as the *decisive crucible where the Christian Bible was formed.*"[66] Consequently, the Bible is in the liturgical assembly as a fish is in water. Scripture, by its very constitution, is meant to be "proclaimed in the assembly, not to be read in a book open flat on the desk in one's office and in an individual manner (whatever the legitimacy and fruitfulness of this practice may be in other respects)."[67] For Chauvet in particular, biblical truth arises from an always unpredictable encounter between the text and the ecclesial community.

But whereas Kavanagh and Chauvet understand Scripture and *liturgy* as two sides of the same coin, Webster argues that one's doctrine of Scripture is inseparable from one's *doctrine of God.* According to this revised understanding, the problem of fundamentalism is less liturgical than it is pneumatological and Christological: it transfers the life and power of the Father directly to the biblical text itself. However, revelation is Trinitarian in nature. The Father is a communicative agent whose Spirit is "mute" without the Word, and whose Word is "inactive" without the Spirit.[68] The Triune God is thus "the epitome of communicative agency: the speech agent who utters, embodies, and keeps his Word."[69] Webster is not advocating a spiritualized ecclesiology, which reduces the interpretation of Scripture to something vastly internal and individualistic. While not denying the significance of the ecclesial community, Webster is adamant that its role is not to *create* biblical meaning, but rather to *discover* and *attest* to its continuing significance.

64. Chauvet, *Symbol and Sacrament*, p. 175.

65. Kavanagh, *On Liturgical Theology*, p. 111.

66. Chauvet, *Symbol and Sacrament*, p. 197.

67. Chauvet, *Symbol and Sacrament*, p. 46.

68. Kevin J. Vanhoozer, *Is There a Meaning in This Text? The Bible, the Reader, and the Morality of Literary Knowledge* (Grand Rapids: Zondervan, 1998), p. 428.

69. Vanhoozer, *Is There a Meaning in This Text?*, p. 457.

Gordon Lathrop and Paul Tillich

Lutheran liturgical scholar Gordon Lathrop is similarly concerned about the effects of biblical fundamentalism on the liturgy. He believes that liturgy offers a middle way through a series of false alternatives:

> It is neither pure biblical criticism nor biblical fundamentalism. It does not gather us around a lecture on the critical interpretation of a biblical book nor into an exercise of communal convictions regarding biblical inerrancy. Rather, the liturgy inserts us into the rich dialectic of the biblical word.[70]

Lathrop draws on the theology of Paul Tillich to explain how this biblical dialectic works. Faith, according to Tillich, has to do with matters of ultimate concern, presented in the form of symbol and myth. In their "unbroken" form, myths are histories that make the religious transcendent perfectly knowable and the workings of the natural world readily explainable.[71] Religion and science are two sides of the same mythical coin. The problem is that humans live in a new, modern age, where religion and science have been irrevocably torn asunder. Humanity's sacred myths no longer seem plausible.

Tillich's solution is not to remove myths from Christian theology. They are, after all, essential modes of encounter with the sacred. Instead, myths must be "broken" — understood *as* myths — without being removed or replaced. Many Christians are afraid of this act of demythologization. They "resist, often fanatically, any attempt to introduce an element of uncertainty by 'breaking the myth,'" and this resistance "frequently expresses itself in the form of literalism."[72] However, Tillich insists that the risk is worth taking. Literalism deprives God of ultimacy and majesty: "Faith, if it takes its symbols literally, becomes idolatrous! It calls something ultimate which is less than ultimate."[73]

---

70. Gordon W. Lathrop, *Holy Things: A Liturgical Theology* (Minneapolis: Fortress Press, 1993), pp. 175-76.

71. Gary Dorrien, *The Word as True Myth: Interpreting Modern Theology* (Louisville: Westminster John Knox Press, 1997), p. 119.

72. Paul Tillich, *Dynamics of Faith* (New York: Harper & Brothers, 1957), p. 51.

73. Tillich, *Dynamics of Faith*, p. 52.

Lathrop builds on Tillich's work to draw a parallel in liturgical studies. According to Tillich, myths are "both true and at the same time wrong, capable of truth only by reference to a new thing beyond its own terms."[74] Lathrop suggests that a similar break is present in the deep intention of the words and ritual practices of the liturgy: "The old is maintained; yet, by means of juxtaposition and metaphor, the old is made to speak the new."[75] Tillich and Lathrop approach Scripture not as a numinous object but rather as a "string of beads" or a "muffin full of berries" — Scripture is "a multitude of more or less discrete units . . . which taken separately and together express the occurrence of a revelatory event."[76]

For example, Lathrop points out that the appointment of the twelve disciples (Mark 3:16; cf. 1 Cor. 15:5) recalls the twelve tribes at Sinai and the setting up of the memorial pillars (Exod. 24:4; Josh. 4:1-7), just as the appointment, mission, and return of the "seventy" (Luke 10:1, 17) recalls the seventy elders of Israel who came up on the mountain with Moses (Exod. 24:1, 9).[77] The Song of the Sea in Exodus 15 leads us on to read the Song of the Arm of the Lord in Isaiah 51:9-11. Through this juxtaposition, it becomes clear that the God who made a way through the sea now makes a way through the desert; the water that once drowned the Egyptians now flows to quench thirst. The biblical rebirth of images is what makes it possible for Paul to compare baptism to the crossing of the sea and the Eucharist to drinking from the rock (1 Cor. 10:1-4).[78] The list could easily continue; however, the point Lathrop wishes to stress is this: "Each occurrence of the symbol, linked together with the earlier uses like a chain of flowers or gems, intensifies the meaning."[79]

The power of this chain of images is that each of its symbols, like the myth to which they collectively point, must be broken. Tillich notes that the symbol "Messiah" is used in the Old Testament to express a hope of a coming military hero who will free his people from political bondage. This symbol is subsequently "broken" in the New Testament — the power of Christ, the

74. Lathrop, *Holy Things*, p. 27.

75. Lathrop, *Holy Things*, p. 27.

76. Kelsey, *The Uses of Scripture in Recent Theology*, p. 56.

77. Gordon Lathrop, *Holy People: A Liturgical Ecclesiology* (Minneapolis: Fortress Press, 1999), p. 36.

78. Lathrop, *Holy People*, p. 39.

79. Lathrop, *Holy People*, p. 32.

powerful liberator, was effective only in the brokenness and weakness of the cross.[80] Lathrop adds other biblical examples: the people who follow Jesus are called "holy ones" and "priests"; the crucified is called "temple"; and God is called "rock," "fire," and "king." The names are "accurate misnaming," "inappropriate in the right direction."[81] These are symbols that effectively engage readers, yet whose limitations are also known.

Once again, there is much in Lathrop's account with which evangelicals can agree. Lathrop insists that the Bible is not understood profoundly enough "if it is thought to be exhausted simply in the presentation of biblical images or the telling of biblical stories, as if presenting a static image were what the gathering was about."[82] Systematic theologian Kevin Vanhoozer concurs: "Mere repetition of the story is not enough, first because repetition does not advance our understanding of the story (e.g., why did Jesus have to die?), and second, because mere repetition does not advance our understanding of how the story bears significantly on the world in which we live."[83]

If not as a presentation of static narratives, how does the Bible function in the ecclesial assembly? According to Lathrop, Scripture and liturgy are especially interested "in sea, in tree, in priests, in fire, or in a hundred other powerful images" — ancient symbols that are made to speak the grace of God anew through their juxtaposition with one another and the Christ-event. Typology becomes "a liturgical figure of speech which is itself revelatory . . . a name for the shift of images which occurs in the assembly, calling us to conversion and faith."[84] To all of this, evangelicals again say a hearty "Amen." In particular, Vanhoozer would appreciate Lathrop's emphasis on typology — a principle that Vanhoozer calls the "mainspring" of biblical unity, the "connecting link between the history of Israel and the history of the church, and the glue that unifies the Old and New Testaments."[85] Vanhoozer cites Luke 24:27 — "Then beginning with Moses and all the prophets, [Jesus] in-

---

80. See Kelsey, *The Uses of Scripture in Recent Theology*, p. 70.

81. Gordon Lathrop, "A Rebirth of Images: On the Use of the Bible in the Liturgy," *Worship* 58 (1984): 293.

82. Lathrop, "A Rebirth of Images," p. 292.

83. Vanhoozer, *The Drama of Doctrine*, p. 95.

84. Lathrop, "A Rebirth of Images," p. 295.

85. Vanhoozer, *The Drama of Doctrine*, p. 223.

terpreted to them the things about himself in all the Scriptures" — to emphasize that "no other canonical practice is more christological than typology."[86]
Furthermore, Vanhoozer aptly observes that the fundamentalist temptation
has been "to regard narrative simply as the pretty packaging of historical
content to be torn off and discarded."[87] Against this position, Vanhoozer
and Lathrop concur that narratives make "story-shaped points that cannot
always be paraphrased in propositional statements without losing something
in translation."[88] Biblical symbols, metaphors, and narratives are irreducible
to propositionalist phrasing.

However, Vanhoozer offers a point of nuance to Lathrop's analysis of
Scripture. Lathrop singles out for special attention the rhetoric of the parables of Jesus. Parables assume "a world determined by old religious speech
— an overarching mythic language of common expectation and meaning
— which is then turned on its head or broken." According to Lathrop, *"the
most central texts of the biblical tradition make use of this pattern."*[89] But
Vanhoozer queries, "Can one approach to reading the Bible do justice to its
literary, historical, and theological variety?"[90] Vanhoozer reminds Lathrop
that while *portions* of Scripture are undeniably comprised of parables, images, and symbols, a robust liturgical theology must also account for the fact
that the Bible is *more* than these things — it is also history, law, command,
and revealed proposition.

This point is significant. Although Vanhoozer has argued that biblical
narratives are not reducible to propositions, he simultaneously insists that
readers "must not leave propositions behind" or reject the idea that Scripture
has determinative content. The instinct of biblical fundamentalism is sound
because the gospel is informative: "He is risen!"[91] Without some propositional core, "the church would be evacuated of its raison d'être, leaving only
programs and potlucks."[92] Harold Best makes a similar point: "Just because

86. Vanhoozer, *The Drama of Doctrine*, p. 221.

87. Vanhoozer, *The Drama of Doctrine*, p. 282.

88. Vanhoozer, *The Drama of Doctrine*, p. 93.

89. Lathrop, *Holy Things*, p. 27.

90. Kevin J. Vanhoozer, *First Theology: God, Scripture, and Hermeneutics* (Downers
Grove, Ill.: InterVarsity Press, 2002), p. 28.

91. Vanhoozer, *First Theology*, p. 278.

92. Vanhoozer, *First Theology*, p. 278.

we are a culture of episodic and experiential narrative does not mean there is no room for the idea, the concept, and the proposition. Otherwise . . . where would the epistles to the Romans and Hebrews be?"[93] These evangelical theologians remind liturgical scholars that to elevate any one biblical literary genre — including that of myth, parable, or symbol — over all others is to "succumb to the same temptation that besets the propositionalist, namely, of reducing the many canonical forms into one kind only."[94]

Conclusion

To better account for diversity within the canon, evangelicals propose their own set of metaphors. Vanhoozer suggests that Scripture is like a collection of diverse maps gathered together in a unified atlas. Some maps highlight the topography of a given region; others tell a person where to find buried treasure. A road atlas renders the world differently than does a political map. In short, every map reflects specific perspectives and serves specific purposes.[95] Similarly, "biblical stories, commands, promises, songs, prophecies, and didactic discourse all mediate God's communicative action, but not all in the same way."[96] Vanhoozer concedes that all scriptural word-maps are not equivalent in what they say or how they say it. However, he adds,

> the various maps of Scripture "fit" together in the sense that each is *compatible* with the other; this means, minimally (and somewhat negatively), that they do not contradict one another. More positively, they share a common *orientation*. Though the various forms of biblical discourse work with different keys and scales, they all render the same kerygma and are all oriented to Jesus Christ, their coordinating compass. If they cohere, it is not because they share the same conceptual space but rather because they are held together in, by, and for Christ.[97]

93. Harold Best, "A Traditional Worship Response," in *Exploring the Worship Spectrum: Six Views,* ed. Paul A. Basden (Grand Rapids: Zondervan, 2004), p. 198.

94. Vanhoozer, *The Drama of Doctrine,* p. 273.

95. Vanhoozer, *The Drama of Doctrine,* p. 297.

96. Vanhoozer, *The Drama of Doctrine,* p. 297.

97. Vanhoozer, *The Drama of Doctrine,* p. 299.

The canon is a unique compass that points to the church's North Star: Jesus Christ.[98]

In a related analogy, Howard Marshall suggests that Scripture is like "a climbing rope that is made up of various strands that are twisted together and run along the length of the rope."[99] Certain theological strands — for example, the belief in one God, creator and ruler of the universe — run the entire length of the rope and are a major locus of its identity and unity. Other strands may not run through the entirety of the rope but still stretch for considerable distances. Examples include the redemptive work of Jesus Christ and the doctrine of the Holy Spirit — although obvious in the latter part of biblical revelation, neither is explicit at most points in the Old Testament. Still other significant strands may be woven in at later stages (e.g., baptism, the Lord's Supper, the notion of the body of Christ), while strands that were once prominent (e.g., ritual prescriptions, food laws, the requirement of physical circumcision) may gradually disappear.[100] Despite these differences in the length of strands, the rope is best conceived as a unity: there is continuity from one part to the next, there are no breaks in it, and the rope can do much the same things at any point in its length.

Although there must be *some* themes present across the entirety of the scriptural rope, not every basic strand runs through each and every passage. Nicholas Wolterstorff offers an example:

> The canon as a whole exhibits the interlocking themes of divine creation, redemption, and consummation; the fact that the book of Ecclesiastes, for example, says nothing about redemption and consummation, but speaks only of God as creator and of our human existence within creation, seems to me to count not at all against that interpretation.[101]

98. Vanhoozer, *The Drama of Doctrine,* p. 297.

99. Howard Marshall, "Climbing Ropes, Ellipses, and Symphonies: The Relation between Biblical and Systematic Theology," in *A Pathway into the Holy Scripture,* ed. Satterthwaite and Wright, p. 208.

100. Marshall, "Climbing Ropes, Ellipses, and Symphonies," p. 208.

101. Nicholas Wolterstorff, "The Unity behind the Canon," in *One Scripture or Many? Canon from Biblical, Theological, and Philosophical Perspectives,* ed. Christine Helmer and Christof Landmesser (New York: Oxford University Press, 2004), p. 222.

Accordingly, biblical scholars must "resist the rigid insistence that each and every book in the canon fully exhibit the unity proposed; no text except the briefest would ever count as unified on that insistence."[102] This is an important lesson for the discipline of liturgical studies. Just as the book of Ecclesiastes is difficult to reconcile with the salvation history perspective of the rest of Scripture, so Eugene Brand points out that "evangelical, holiness, Pentecostal, and independent charismatic movements"[103] pose problems for the sacramental understanding of Christianity. Yet Ecclesiastes shares enough theological similarities with the rest of Scripture to be included as a valued part of the canon. Similarly, Peter Hocken reminds his colleagues in the ecumenical movement that "the 'others' whose theologies and practices pose such problems to our understandings of Christianity and Church acknowledge the foundational Christian truths of incarnation, redemption, and Trinity."[104] Given this recognition, perhaps Marshall's insight can be transposed for the purposes of this chapter: Although there must be *some* theological themes present across the entirety of the liturgical rope, this does not mean that *all* the basic strands (including sacramental ones) must run through each and every worshipping tradition.

Of course, no single analogy, including that of a climbing rope, is without flaws. What are the grounds for believing that liturgical history is more like one rope than several separate lengths tied together at various points, or a number of pieces laid loosely side by side? Are there points where we seem to be dealing with different or broken ropes rather than with the multicolored strands of the same rope? Have there been moments in history when the churches have inserted alien strands into the rope or cut off genuine ones?[105] These important questions are the subject of Chapter Four.

---

102. Wolterstorff, "The Unity behind the Canon," p. 222.

103. Eugene Brand, "Berakah Response: Ecumenism and the Liturgy," *Worship* 58 (1984): 312.

104. Peter Hocken, "Ecumenical Dialogue: The Importance of Dialogue with Evangelicals and Pentecostals," *One in Christ* 30 (1994): 106.

105. Marshall, "Climbing Ropes, Ellipses, and Symphonies," pp. 209-11.

Gnostic versus Canonical?
Rethinking Interpretive Paradigms

We cannot make up just any order, or center the meeting on our own brilliant ideas or techniques, without tearing the church apart.

Gordon Lathrop, *Holy Ground*

Spare no effort! The Spirit indwelling a Catholic is the same Spirit indwelling a Baptist is the same Spirit indwelling someone from our congregation. We're already united.

Pastor Marc Erikson, Eastbrook Church

Throughout this project, I have been calling for a historical and theological understanding of evangelicalism in liturgical studies that will allow the movement to move beyond perceived academic dichotomies. The legacy of George Whitefield — a reformer who encouraged Christians to identify themselves primarily as members of a large ecumenical family and only secondarily as members of a particular denomination — is a critical element of this understanding. As a result, there are two distinct approaches to ecumenism: whereas the liturgical renewal movement grounds the unity of the church in sacramental practices, the heirs of Whitefield discern unity on the basis of the experience of "new birth." Debates in biblical studies have further exacerbated ecumenical tensions: whereas liturgical scholars press for the historical priority of tradition, evangelical scholars argue for the theological priority of Scripture, understood as the medium of Triune self-communication.

In his comparative work on Catholic, Orthodox, and Free Church ecclesiology, theologian Miroslav Volf puts his finger on the crux of a third significant debate. Volf notes that according to the episcopal tradition, "the church is constituted through the performance of objective activities," which include the actions of the bishops who administer the sacraments and the actions of the laity who fully participate in liturgical life. Accordingly, most post–Vatican II liturgical scholarship stresses that it is the Eucharist that makes the church and the church that makes the Eucharist. For example, Gordon Lathrop writes that "an ecclesiology according to the Eucharist is exactly what is needed for reflection upon church"; and Simon Chan asserts, "The worship of the church is essentially eucharistic because it is the Eucharist that makes the church uniquely what it is. . . . Eucharist is the supreme expression of the worship that realizes the church."[1] In contrast, Free Churches "have come to emphasize subjective conditions — namely, faith and obedience — to the point that where these are missing, even if the objective side is present, a serious doubt arises concerning ecclesiality."[2] It is this tension between the "objective" and "subjective" constitution of the church that lies at the heart of this chapter.

Perhaps the most problematic charge that liturgical scholars level against evangelicalism is that nonsacramental worship celebrates individuals and their processes of decision-making instead of the Triune God. More often than not, a second charge follows on the heels of the first: evangelical worship is more "gnostic" (concerned with salvation and the escape of the fleshly conditions of life) than it is "Christian." For example, Frank Senn maintains that Jonathan Edwards remained "within the orbit of historical Christianity," but that Charles Finney should be "associated with the peculiarly American kind of Gnosticism that finds salvation in knowledge, especially in knowing how to do something."[3]

---

1. Gordon Lathrop, *Holy People: A Liturgical Ecclesiology* (Minneapolis: Fortress Press, 1999), pp. 15-16; and Simon Chan, *Liturgical Theology: The Church as Worshiping Community* (Downers Grove, Ill.: IVP Academic, 2006), pp. 71-72.

2. Veli-Matti Kärkkäinen, *An Introduction to Ecclesiology: Ecumenical, Historical, and Global Perspectives* (Downers Grove, Ill.: InterVarsity Press, 2002), p. 136.

3. Frank Senn, "'Worship Alive': An Analysis and Critique of 'Alternative Worship,'" *Worship* 69, no. 3 (1995): 204.

Because this contrast has been especially prominent in the work of Lutheran liturgical scholar Gordon Lathrop, I begin the chapter with an overview of his thought. I then argue that we need a more theologically nuanced statement of evangelical soteriology. To this end, I introduce the work of systematic theologian Miroslav Volf, whose book *After Our Likeness* remains one of the most significant statements of Free Church ecclesiology. As a result of the conversation between Volf and Lathrop, it becomes clear that a new evangelical-ecumenical paradigm is needed. I conclude by suggesting that evangelical ecclesiology is more closely aligned with the Fourth Gospel than with early gnostic heresies, and that, in fact, the Johannine/Synoptic relationship provides a promising ecumenical lens for understanding evangelicalism's relation to liturgical Christianity.

Gordon Lathrop and the Ecumenical *Ordo*

Gordon Lathrop's trilogy of books, *Holy Things, Holy People,* and *Holy Ground,* have been lauded as groundbreaking works of liturgical theology. In these volumes, Lathrop emphasizes the "primary things" of bath, word, table, and prayer as the dominant proposal for liturgical unity in contemporary liturgical theology. These elements take on meaning in action; indeed, it is their juxtaposition that makes for the Christian distinctiveness of the liturgical event. At the heart of Lathrop's work is the Lutheran dialectic of law and gospel. Liturgy is always "a welcome to *here* that is always open to *there,*" always an invitation paired with a warning — "holy things for the holy people."[4] Lathrop explains that juxtaposition is the key characteristic of the *ordo* because "Christian worship speaks truthfully about God by always speaking at least two words, two things together."[5]

One of the pairings upon which Lathrop is most insistent is that of word and table. Lathrop finds evidence for this juxtaposition in the second-century writings of Justin Martyr and across all four first-century Gospels. He stresses,

---

4. Gordon Lathrop, *Holy Things: A Liturgical Theology* (Minneapolis: Fortress Press, 1993), p. 121.

5. Lathrop, *Holy Things,* p. 121.

This twofold pattern of the assembly has been called by a variety of names in the Christian East and West, but it has been universal. Even when the *ordo* has decayed, as in the loss of preaching or of vernacular scripture reading among Roman Catholics and the Orthodox, or, as in the disappearance of the weekly meal among Western Protestants, the resultant liturgical practice has often been accompanied by a memory that the full twofold action was the classic Christian norm for Sunday.[6]

Lathrop's expectation of scriptural word juxtaposed to thanksgiving meal ought not to be misconstrued as a demand for imposed uniformity. The *ordo* is a gift to be celebrated, not a law to be enforced. Furthermore, the *ordo* can be done in many different languages, using a rich variety of song and hymnody, with varying degrees of ceremony, in architectural splendor or open air. Yet within this diversity of local celebrations, Lathrop underscores the ecumenical unity found in the deep structure of bath, word, prayer, and table — herein lies an apostolic *ordo* that forms "the inheritance of all the churches, founded in the New Testament, locally practiced today, and attested to in the ancient sources of both the Christian East and the Christian West."[7]

However, for the evangelicals I am studying, Lathrop's expectation of a weekly juxtaposition between word and table across all Christian traditions sets the minimum standard of ecumenism too high. Lathrop acknowledges that it is possible to read with some sympathy the history of those who incorporated protests into the assembly: for example, Quakers and Salvationists, who do not keep bath or table; Baptists and Mennonites, who welcome only the confessing adult members of the assembly to the bath; and feminists, who must "sometimes lock the door when the liturgy hopes to safely welcome abused women to a celebration of honesty and healing."[8] Lathrop labels these movements "catholic exceptions" to the ecumenical *ordo*: they function as prophetic outsiders vis-à-vis the liturgical churches, and their protests are important for the overall health of the Christian faith.[9] Simultaneously, these

6. Lathrop, *Holy Things*, p. 51.

7. Lathrop, *Holy People*, p. 231.

8. Gordon Lathrop, *Holy Ground: A Liturgical Cosmology* (Minneapolis: Fortress Press, 2003), p. 226.

9. Gordon Lathrop, *Holy Things*, pp. 157-58.

catholic exceptions are "challenged and enriched by the presence of the *ordo* in other places — by the invitation to join, at least sometimes, in the ritual symbol that they want their lives to enact."[10]

But Lathrop's comments regarding catholic exceptions are problematic in two ways. First, determining what is "catholic" and what is "exception" has the potential to be a highly contentious exercise. Upon what grounds does one make this normative judgment? Scripture? Tradition? Such questions quickly rise to the fore in ecumenical discussions of baptism. Lathrop is clear that

> the baptismal events follow this pattern: we teach and then we wash. The Christian faith includes a tradition that must be learned, scriptures to read, questions to ask about one's life, names with which to interpret the world, prayers to pray, an ordering or scheduling to take on as one's own. All of this precedes the bath.[11]

Therefore, it is curious that he includes "Baptists and Mennonites [who] welcome only the confessing, adult members of the assembly to the bath" as examples of catholic exceptions to the *ordo*.[12] The World Council of Church's convergence statement in *Baptism, Eucharist, and Ministry* reminds readers that baptism upon a personal profession of faith is the most clearly attested pattern in the New Testament. While the possibility of infant baptism from the apostolic age cannot be excluded, the Lima text clearly suggests that it is *adult* baptism that serves as a model. Hence, what one ecclesial tradition deems "catholic" on historical grounds (infant baptism) might just as validly be considered a scriptural "exception" in another ecclesial tradition.[13]

---

10. Gordon Lathrop, "Bath, Word, Prayer, Table: Reflections on Doing the Liturgical *Ordo* in a Postmodern Time," in *Ordo: Bath, Word, Prayer, Table — A Liturgical Primer in Honor of Gordon W. Lathrop*, ed. Dirk G. Lange and Dwight W. Vogel (Akron: OSL Publications, 2005), p. 226.

11. Lathrop, *Holy Things*, p. 59.

12. Lathrop, *Holy Ground*, p. 225.

13. In his writings on the Rite of Christian Initiation of Adults, Aidan Kavanagh goes so far as to suggest that infant baptism is a "benign abnormality": "The conciliar emphasis is clearly on the adult nature of the norm of Christian initiation, deriving as it does from the New Testament doctrine of conversion. . . . The baptism of adults as the norm throws infant

Second, Lathrop's definition of "catholic exceptions" as those "who incorporate protests into the assembly" does not account for the fact that most churches who follow alternative *ordos* are, quite simply, not protesting anything. As Avery Dulles correctly notes, "Evangelicals are not, as a group, anti-sacramental. Many of them, conceding that the Church has from the beginning practiced sacramental worship, contend that such practice should continue."[14] Although not all Free Church congregations celebrate the Lord's Supper weekly, they find no fault with — indeed, they recognize, support, and encourage — those Christian traditions that do. Christopher Ellis explains:

> [In Baptist worship] the *ordo,* and in particular the "and" between word and meal, may stretch over a wider time span than the gathering and dismissal each Sunday. What is being argued is not that weekly celebration is in any way inappropriate, or that it doesn't express the *ordo,* but that it is not the *only* expression of an *ordo* where word and table are "in apposition," where the Sunday gathering is "a communal meeting around two poles."[15]

In short, the groups Lathrop labels as "catholic exceptions" do not wish to be "tolerated and footnoted as some sort of Christian aberration."[16] This is because, in Steffen Lösel's apt summation, they "ultimately understand themselves to be part of a fully valid expression of Christianity, not of insufficient parts or institutionalized critical principles that only function as a corrective of others."[17]

---

baptism into perspective as a benign abnormality as long as it is practiced with prudence as an unavoidable pastoral necessity" (*The Shape of Baptism: The Rite of Christian Initiation* [Yonkers, N.Y.: Pueblo Publishing Co., 1978], p. 110).

14. Avery Dulles, "Church, Ministry, and Sacraments in Catholic-Evangelical Dialogue," in *Catholics and Evangelicals: Do They Share a Common Future?*, ed. Thomas Rausch (New York: Paulist Press, 2000), p. 110.

15. Christopher Ellis, *Gathering: A Theology and Spirituality of Worship in Free Church Tradition* (London: SCM Press), p. 254.

16. This is the objection of Quaker theologian Eden Grace. See "Reflections on What Quakers Bring to the Ecumenical Table," at http://www.edengrace.org/sacraments.htm.

17. Steffen Lösel, "What Sacred Symbols Say about Strangers and Strawberries: Gordon W. Lathrop's Liturgical Theology in Review," *Journal of Religion* 85, no. 4 (2005): 647.

If Lathrop's first explanation of non-*ordo* churches as "catholic exceptions" is problematic, his second proposal is more troubling. Lathrop hints that if the ecumenical *ordo* represents a commitment to go the way of "the [four canonical] gospels of baptism, word, meal, and sending," then the threefold Frontier *ordo* outlined in Chapter One is more closely aligned with gnostic-discourse gospels.[18] Lathrop argues that the deep structure of the ecumenical *ordo* comes directly from the pattern of the New Testament Gospels: Mark "moves from the baptism of Jesus to the collected stories and sayings of Jesus to the meal (or meals) which show forth the meaning of the passion, to the passion itself, to the ending which sends the reading community back to the beginning of the book again."[19] Matthew and Luke add infancy narratives, and John adds a prologue; however, these also "follow exactly the same shape: baptism, narratives, meal and passion, resurrection and sending."[20] Although there is no way to know why the Markan form became normative, Lathrop suggests a reciprocal relationship: perhaps the Gospels provided a manual and common shape for Christian practice, or Christian practice gave shape to the Gospel books. In any case, *ordo* and the shape of the canonical Gospels have been foundationally intertwined from the very beginning of the church.

By contrast, gnostic-discourse gospels evidence a noticeably different shape. They begin after the Resurrection; their concern is to help individual souls escape the world. Instead of faith, their emphasis is on *askesis* (technique), which enables the self to escape the fleshly conditions of life for salvational fulfillment.[21] In Lathrop's assessment, certain characteristics of the Frontier tradition align it more closely with gnostic than New Testament traditions. He explains:

The danger of this widespread and influential [evangelical megachurch] pattern should now be clear, however. Its characteristics — only a little Scripture, and that mostly Scripture verses with an accent on technique; the importance of the individual; no meal; little sense of assembly — place

18. Gordon Lathrop, "Worship in the Twenty-First Century: Ordo," in *Currents in Theology and Mission* 26, no. 4 (1999): 300.
19. Lathrop, *Holy Ground*, p. 147.
20. Lathrop, *Holy Ground*, p. 147.
21. Lathrop, "Worship in the Twenty-First Century: Ordo," p. 293.

it far closer to the discourse gospels, to the old sacrophobic way, than to the assemblies of the four gospels of the New Testament. This *ordo* can easily support, without challenge or transformation, American individualism and the gnostic tendency of American religion.[22]

Certainly evangelicals with ties to the Frontier *ordo* have strong reasons to object to Lathrop's assessment. In his theological summary of the *Gospel of Thomas*, Richard Valantasis explains this gnostic work is comprised of post-Resurrection collections of the sayings of Jesus, generally understood as revealed to individuals. The sayings challenge, puzzle, and sometimes even provide conflicting information about a given subject. Because the topics shift rapidly, with little meaningful connection between them, the audience is cajoled into "thinking, experiencing, processing information, and responding to important issues of life and living without more than a brief time to consider the question fully." This results in an unusual kind of assembly:

> The community developed in this gospel is not one analogous to a parish, or a church, or any other organized group of people with a structure and a charter. Rather, this community is a loose confederation of people who have independently related the sayings and found their interpretation, who have begun to perform the actions that inaugurate the new identity, and who have become capable of seeing other people who perform similar activities. The community, in short, is a by-product of the theological mode, a loose conglomeration of people of similar mentality and ways of living, but who do not necessarily live together as an intentional community.[23]

Is it fair to claim that the "community" elicited by a reading of the *Gospel of Thomas* is analogous to the assembly of a megachurch congregation? A more nuanced assessment of evangelical thought is required, and to this end, I turn to the work of Miroslav Volf.

---

22. Lathrop, *Holy Ground,* p. 140.
23. Richard Valantasis, *The Gospel of Thomas* (New York: Routledge, 1997), p. 7.

Miroslav Volf

In his book *After Our Likeness*, theologian Miroslav Volf outlines a Trinitarian ecclesiology in critical interaction between Roman Catholic, Orthodox, and Free Church ecclesiology.[24] Ecclesiologists concur that this book is "one of the first theologically responsible, constructive works from a Free Church perspective."[25] In what follows, I draw selectively from Volf's work and put it in conversation with Lathrop's theology to parse more precisely what evangelicals mean when they speak of "personal faith."

Volf and Lathrop share many commitments, especially given the fact that Volf identifies "a vision of spiritual life that needs to be liturgically celebrated and also prayed, fasted, and lived out communally" as the heart of his proposal.[26] Volf's definition of the church begins with Matthew 18:20: "where two or three are gathered in my name, I am there among them" (NRSV). The church is first and foremost an assembly of people gathered *in Jesus' name*. Lathrop rightly points out that it is all too easy to make "the name of Jesus" — a name that has currently become synonymous with popular religion — merely a projection of our own ideals.[27] This is why Volf stresses that ecclesiality in the name of Christ must be "dependent upon certain doctrinal specifications."[28] He explains:

> One can relate to Jesus Christ only by believing *something* about him. The content of faith is necessary in order to distinguish Jesus Christ from "another Jesus" and to distinguish his Spirit from "another Spirit" (see 2 Cor. 11:4). . . . To be sure, doctrine is not an end in itself, but rather merely a means of preserving and fostering the relation between the assembled congregation and Jesus Christ. It serves to identify unequivocally the person in whose name the congregation gathers.[29]

24. For an overview of Volf, see Kärkkäinen, *An Introduction to Ecclesiology*, pp. 134-41.

25. Kärkkäinen, *An Introduction to Ecclesiology*, p. 135.

26. See Miroslav Volf, "Miroslav Volf Replies," *Conrad Grebel Review* 18, no. 3 (2000): 63-66.

27. See Lathrop, *Holy People*, p. 111.

28. Miroslav Volf, *After Our Likeness: The Church as the Image of the Trinity* (Grand Rapids: Wm. B. Eerdmans, 1998), p. 146.

29. Volf, *After Our Likeness*, p. 146.

Volf's emphasis on doctrinal specifications might not sit easily with Lathrop. Acknowledging that it "would not be wrong" to answer the question about the mutual recognition of churches by inquiring about doctrine, Lathrop worries that in so doing, we might easily forget that "doctrine is first of all what we teach and confess and enact in Baptism," and that "primary theology is found in the preaching, prayers, and communal actions of the Eucharist."[30] Against this view, Paul Bradshaw finds it highly doubtful that worshippers ever engage in acts of *pure* primary theology like those Lathrop describes: "When Christians gather on a Sunday morning to worship God," Bradshaw points out, "they do not come with their minds a *tabula rasa*. On the contrary, they come with their religious attitudes and expectations already formed by secondary theology, as a result of that catechesis that their particular ecclesiastical tradition has given them over the years."[31] There is something "existentially prior" to the liturgical act — and it is this "something" that Volf defines as "the confession of faith."

A word of clarification is in order. To embrace Volf's emphasis on the priority of a confession of faith is not to subscribe to the bleak scenario that Aidan Kavanagh paints, wherein liturgy becomes an educational event in which "the merely baptized" are "expected to bring their study texts — their Bibles, prayerbooks, and layfolk's missals — with them and to sit, school-room fashion, in rows of linotypical pews and be instructed."[32] By "confession of faith," Volf has in mind something similar to Lathrop's decision to name the central things of worship as "meeting, gathering, book, song, and speech" rather than "divine service, evangelary, baptism, Holy Eucharist, offertory, and sermon."[33] Lathrop explains that the latter are "good words, but they already evidence layers of interpretation that can, for many, too easily become layers of mystification."[34]

"Justification," "sanctification," and "atonement" are good theological words as well. However, Volf notes that doctrinal confessions of faith may also be quite simple and brief (i.e., "Jesus is Lord") and may well vary, as they

---

30. Lathrop, *Holy People*, p. 122.

31. Paul Bradshaw, "Difficulties in Doing Liturgical Theology," *Pacifica* 11 (1998): 191.

32. Aidan Kavanagh, *On Liturgical Theology* (Yonkers, N.Y.: Pueblo Publishing Co., 1992), p. 111.

33. Lathrop, *Holy People*, pp. 10-11.

34. Lathrop, *Holy People*, p. 11.

did in the New Testament. A confession of faith "consists less in verbalizing a particular theological content than in acknowledging him whom the content of the confession is identifying."[35] He explains,

> Without personal identification with Jesus Christ, cognitive specification of who he is remains empty; without cognitive specification of who Jesus Christ is, however, personal identification with him is blind. In the act of *confessing faith,* this cognitive speculation and personal identification coincide.[36]

Every genuine Christian speech act — including the celebration of the sacraments, sermons, prayer, hymns, witnessing, and daily life — is a form of confession by which those gathered in the name of Christ speak the word of God to one another and the world.

Volf's connection between the act of confessing faith and the celebration of the sacraments leads directly to the point that Lathrop has identified as "the center of the disagreement between the megachurches and classic, ecumenical Christianity: the question of *means.*"[37] Because the unresolved issues are so important, Lathrop's summary of them is worth quoting at length:

> Is the church centered on individuals and their processes of decision-making? Or is it centered on — indeed, created by — certain concrete and communal means which God has given, which bear witness to and give the grace of God and in which God is present? That is the question. It will not do to answer that the megachurches have sacraments. So did the camp meetings. But the sacraments can be so fenced or so individualized or so transformed into signs of human decision that they yield the ecclesial center of attention to the processes of decision-making. . . . From the classic Christian point of view, if decision-making is the central matter, the meeting will not really be around God, no matter how orthodox or trinitarian a theology may be in the mind of the "speaker."[38]

35. Volf, *After Our Likeness,* p. 149.
36. Volf, *After Our Likeness,* p. 148.
37. Gordon Lathrop, "New Pentecost or Joseph's Britches? Reflections on the History and Meaning of the Worship Ordo in the Megachurches," *Worship* 6 (2001): 533.
38. Lathrop, "New Pentecost or Joseph's Britches?," p. 533.

Any response to Lathrop must begin by addressing his concerns about the prominence of "human decision-making" in evangelical churches. The vast majority of Free Churches unreservedly affirm the ecumenical consensus that faith is strictly a work of God's Spirit and God's word. No one can give oneself faith, and Volf is unambiguous in his insistence that "it is *God* who opens the hearts to the Gospel, *God* who kills the old self and makes alive the new, *God* who comes to dwell in the soul."[39]

At the same time, Volf points to an element of human volition in the act of faith, evidenced, for example, in Mary's response to the angel in Luke 1:38: "Here am I, the servant of the Lord; let it be with me according to your word." In recognizing human volition, Volf does not suggest that faith is simply a "free deed of decision." Rather, he is asserting that human passivity is a "*responsorial* passivity of letting oneself be," and that this act of "letting oneself be" is "inconceivable without the will." Put differently, although faith is exclusively a gift from God, "the believing 'yes' to God, a 'yes' that must be pronounced by the self and nobody else, is soteriologically indispensable."[40]

Following this logic, the decision that Lathrop has placed before evangelicals — a choice between the church as established by the decisions of individuals or the church as established by divinely instituted means of grace — posits an unnecessary, even erroneous, dichotomy. Free Churches refuse to privilege one option over the other because they believe *both* are simultaneously true. On the one hand, Volf concurs with Lathrop that sacraments belong to the *esse* of the church: "There does not seem to have been any initial period in church history without baptism or the Lord's Supper."[41] Furthermore, it is "the Spirit of God, acting through the word of God and the sacraments," who constitutes the church. On the other hand, Free Churches are equally insistent that it is *individuals* who "accept the gifts of God in faith (even if this faith is itself a gift of God.)"[42] Baptism and the Lord's Supper "can be an indispensable condition of ecclesiality only if they are a form of the confession of faith and an expression of faith."[43] In Volf's summation,

---

39. Miroslav Volf, "Against a Pretentious Church: A Rejoinder to Bell's Response," *Modern Theology* 19 (2003): 283.

40. Volf, *After Our Likeness*, p. 164.

41. Volf, *After Our Likeness*, p. 152.

42. Volf, *After Our Likeness*, p. 176.

43. Volf, *After Our Likeness*, p. 152.

"There is no church without sacraments; but there are no sacraments without the confession of faith and without faith itself."[44]

If not via the *ordo,* upon what other grounds might relations between the churches be established? Volf's minimal requirement is the *openness* of each church to all other churches that make a confession of faith. This common confession connects every church with all others: by isolating itself, a church "attests either that it is professing faith in 'a different Christ' than [other congregations] or is denying in practice the *common* Jesus Christ to whom it professes faith."[45] In Volf's words, "A church that closes itself off from other churches of God past or present, or a church that has no desire to turn to these churches in some fashion, is denying its own catholicity."[46]

This "obligation to openness" as a minimum of catholicity helps protect Free Churches (with their emphasis on the autonomy of local congregations and the biblical principle of "two or three" gathered in Christ's name) from falling prey to the very real dangers of particularism and special interests. Furthermore, Volf stresses that "it would be a mistake to confuse the minimum of catholicity with its optimum":

> Although a church that were *only* open to all other churches would indeed be a catholic church, it would clearly be a *poor* catholic church. Every catholic church is charged with maintaining and deepening its ties to other churches past and present. . . . Openness to other churches should lead to a free networking with those churches, and as the image of the net also suggests, these mutual relations should be expressed in corresponding ecclesial institutions.[47]

This means that Christians have every reason to celebrate the ecumenical and liturgical advances of the past several decades: advances that have, in Bradshaw's apt summary, helped the churches "[recover] important emphases and insights from our earlier heritage that we had lost in the course of more recent centuries" and "[gain] a much broader vision of the nature of

44. Volf, *After Our Likeness,* p. 154.
45. Volf, *After Our Likeness,* p. 157.
46. Volf, *After Our Likeness,* p. 275.
47. Volf, *After Our Likeness,* p. 275.

Christianity by sharing in some of the liturgical traditions that belonged to other churches."[48]

However, the "obligation to openness" as a minimum requirement of catholicity works both ways. Liturgical scholars too must be open to the insights and contributions of churches that have *not* actively participated in the liturgical renewal movement. Recalling the categories of the previous chapter, liturgical scholars have too often dismissed non-*ordo* churches as alien strands that have been inserted into the rope of liturgical history. The task of the next section will be to show that liturgical and evangelical strands have from the beginning been intertwined. I will do so by suggesting that Free Church ecclesiology shares more with the Gospel of John than the gnostic *Gospel of Thomas* and, furthermore, that the Johannine-Synoptic relationship holds significant ecumenical potential for understanding the liturgical/evangelical relationship.

John and the Synoptics

Throughout his writings, Lathrop emphasizes that Christians read four Gospels that witness to the one God. Indeed, in James Dunn's words, the fact that the New Testament canonizes no less than four Gospels remains an astonishing fact, too little appreciated because of its familiarity:

> That the early churches were aware of the theological implications and potential problems of embracing four Gospels is sufficiently indicated by the titles that became attached to the four: not "The Gospel *of* Matthew," and so on, as though there were indeed four different gospels, but the gospel "according to [κατά] Matthew," and so on, indicating that the four Gospels are but four versions of the one Gospel. . . . [The] κατά-formulation in a book's title was highly unusual for this period, so we may deduce that the choice of terms was deliberate and constituted a deliberate theological assertion.[49]

---

48. Paul F. Bradshaw, "The Homogenization of Christian Liturgy — Ancient and Modern," *Studia Liturgica* 26 (1996): 13.

49. James D. G. Dunn, "John and the Synoptics as a Theological Question," in *Exploring the Gospel of John* (Louisville: Westminster John Knox Press, 1996), p. 307.

The plurality of the Gospels is a theological issue, made particularly complex by the relationship between John and the Synoptics. "Synoptic" is the Greek word meaning "having one view," and Dunn notes that although a clear interrelationship can readily be discerned among the first three Gospels, "the quantum leap from the Synoptics to John seems to speak more of discontinuity than continuity."[50] The Fourth Gospel is, in Robert Kysar's apt phrase, a "maverick" among the Gospels. It overlaps with the Synoptics in only about 10 percent of its material, runs free of the perspective presented in Matthew, Mark, and Luke, and has been dubbed the "nonconformist Gospel of the bunch."[51] In short, John represents an "adventuresome Christianity" that "freely goes its own way and explores new avenues of expression" without seeking consistency with any other form of early Christian thought.[52] In what follows, it will become clear that this "maverick Gospel" shares strong affinities with Free Church ecclesiology.

It was, in fact, Catholic biblical scholar Raymond Brown who first drew the evangelical-Johannine parallel. In the preface to his work *The Churches the Apostles Left Behind,* Brown notes that Peter, Paul, and James all died in the decade of the 60s, leaving the early churches to carry on without the authoritative guidance of the apostles who had seen the risen Jesus. For this reason, "the New Testament works written after the death of the apostles illustrate different emphases that enabled the respective communities addressed by those works to survive."[53] Both the Pauline and Jerusalem churches followed a familiar sociological sequence: they transitioned from a first-generation community that was enthusiastic, loosely structured, and innovative to a second-generation community with a developing hierarchical structure and a growing consciousness of the need to preserve tradition.

However, the Johannine community functioned differently. Because it was a much more loosely organized and spontaneous group, "neither the sacraments nor the concept of church structure lie at the heart of the Johannine

---

50. Dunn, "John and the Synoptics as a Theological Question," p. 302.

51. Robert Kysar, *John, the Maverick Gospel* (Louisville: Westminster John Knox Press, 1993), p. 2.

52. Kysar, *John, the Maverick Gospel,* p. 131.

53. Raymond E. Brown, *The Churches the Apostles Left Behind* (New York: Paulist Press, 1984), p. 1.

community's concept of itself."[54] In John's Gospel, as in many evangelical churches, liturgy and ecclesiology are subservient to the person of Jesus and a personal relationship with him. The word "church" does not appear in Johannine literature except in 3 John 6, 9, and 10, and even then the emphasis on the relationship of Jesus with "his own" outweighs it.[55] At least three distinctive similarities reinforce the Johannine–Free Church parallel:

1. *The Emphasis on Personal Faith.* Brown observes that near the end of the first century, New Testament writers were picturing Jesus as the builder, founder, or cornerstone of the church (Matt. 16:18; Eph. 2:20). Although this imagery contains important insights, it suffers from limitations. The builder of a standing edifice "did his work in the past; he is present only as a memory." A cornerstone "is necessary in the construction if the building is going to stand; but it is inert, and no one thinks much about its presence once the building is dedicated."[56] Colossians/Ephesians employs a different metaphor: members of the body receive life from Christ the head and are knit together in life with him. This imagery is abstract and impersonal: it does not satisfy the longing to encounter God in a *personal* way.

By contrast, the Fourth Gospel presents an unparalleled concentration on the relation of the individual believer to Jesus, beautifully illustrated in the parables of the Good Shepherd and the vine and branches. In John 10, Jesus speaks of himself as the shepherd of a flock: he knows the sheep that belong to him, he calls each by name, and he will gladly give his life for any one of them. This image is also found in each of the Synoptics (Mark 14:27; Matt. 18:12-24; and Luke 12:32, 15:3-7). However, unique to John is the reciprocal relationship between Jesus and the individual sheep, grounded on the union and relationship between Jesus and his Father.[57] The relation between Jesus and the sheep is described as a mutual *"gnōskein"* — a relationship in which the two partners are by nature bound together. The point of the parable "is the emphasis on the personal knowledge and adherence to Jesus and not on

---

54. Johan Ferreira, *Johannine Ecclesiology* (Sheffield: Sheffield Academic Press, 1998), p. 44.

55. J.-M. R. Tillard, *Church of Churches: The Ecclesiology of Communion* (Collegeville, Minn.: Liturgical Press, 1992), p. 127, n. 123.

56. Brown, *The Churches the Apostles Left Behind*, pp. 86-87.

57. John F. O'Grady, *According to John: The Witness of the Beloved Disciple* (New York: Paulist Press, 1999), p. 44.

the flock as a community."[58] The passage by no means denies a communal aspect to faith: "flock" is a collective image. However, "flock" is made possible "only in and through the response of faith made by the individual in the collectivity."[59]

A similar rhetorical device is at work in the parable of the vine and branches found in John 15. Although all branches must be *individually* attached to the vine of Christ, no consideration is paid to the relationship *between* them. The difference between John's ecclesiological picture and Paul's metaphor of the body of Christ is striking. In 1 Corinthians 12, Paul writes, "As it is, there are many members, yet one body. The eye cannot say to the hand, 'I have no need of you,' nor again the head to the feet, 'I have no need of you.'" In contrast, John 15:6 warns of the possibility that some branches may be cast off and wither and be thrown into the fire. Yet this does not seem to have any effect on the other branches who remain in Jesus (except, perhaps, to serve as a cautionary tale).[60] The sense of mutual interdependence in belonging to Christ — so strong in Paul — is lacking in John. Although "vine and branches" and "sheep gathered into a flock" make up unified realities, they present "a far different image of collectivity than an image that sees each member dependent *on the other* as well as on the source of the communal life."[61]

At this point, a word of caution is in order. I have been stressing the "individualism" of the Fourth Gospel since, as Cambridge scholar C. F. D. Moule has noted, John is "the Gospel, *par excellence,* of the approach of the single soul to God: this is the part of Scripture to which one turns first when trying to direct an enquirer to his own, personal appropriation of salvation."[62] However, Raymond Brown emphasizes the Old Testament and Jewish roots of John: in Christ, God saved *a people.*[63] Indeed, both "flock

58. John F. O'Grady, "Individualism and Johannine Ecclesiology," *Biblical Theology Bulletin* 5 (1975): 242.

59. John F. O'Grady, "Johannine Ecclesiology: A Critical Evaluation," *Biblical Theology Bulletin* 7 (1977): 40.

60. O'Grady, "Individualism and Johannine Ecclesiology," p. 244.

61. O'Grady, "Individualism and Johannine Ecclesiology," p. 244; emphasis mine.

62. C. F. D. Moule, "Individualism of the Fourth Gospel," *Novum Testamentum* 5, no. 2-3 (1962): 185.

63. Brown, *The Churches the Apostles Left Behind,* p. 82.

of sheep" and "branches of a vine" are established images of God's people Israel (Ezek. 34; Ps. 80). Furthermore, much Johannine scholarship takes seriously the possibility that many apparently individual characters in John are in fact representative. The collectivity of salvation is also reinforced in John 10:16, where Jesus says, "I have other sheep that are not of this sheep pen. I must bring them also. They too will listen to my voice, and there shall be one flock and one shepherd." Here Jesus is not talking about individuals but about groups of people.[64]

Thus, Charles Cosgrove is right to nuance the understanding of John as the "individualistic" Gospel: "What should be emphasized is that in John the irreplaceable decision of the individual is a decision for Life *only* if it includes identification with the community in which Jesus and the Father make their present home through the medium of the Spirit."[65] Similarly, John Robinson cautions that the Johannine sense of community and *koinonia* (especially 1 John 3, 6) is stronger than that of any New Testament writer except for Paul. It is therefore more accurate to speak about the "personalism" than the "individualism" of the Fourth Gospel, just as it is more accurate to speak about the "irreducible individual — *not individualistic or autonomous* — element" that lies at the core of evangelicalism.[66]

2. *The De-Emphasis of Hierarchical Offices.* Brown observes that "there is much in Johannine theology that would relativize the importance of institution and office at the very time when their importance was being accentuated in other Christian communities."[67] For example, Matthew envisions a church "built upon Peter in which Peter and the Twelve have the power to bind and to loose" (16:19; 18:18), and Luke/Acts describes "the Twelve at the origins of

---

64. John E. Staton, "A Vision of Unity — Christian Unity in the Fourth Gospel," *Evangelical Quarterly* 69 (1997): 303.

65. Charles H. Cosgrove, "The Place Where Jesus Is: Allusions to Baptism and the Eucharist in the Fourth Gospel," *New Testament Studies* 35, no. 4 (1989): 533, n. 1; emphasis mine.

66. John A. T. Robinson and J. F. Coakley, *The Priority of John* (London: SCM Press, 1985), p. 329; and Roger E. Olson, "Free Church Ecclesiology and Evangelical Spirituality: A Unique Compatibility," in *Evangelical Ecclesiology: Reality or Illusion?*, ed. John G. Stackhouse Jr. (Grand Rapids: Baker Academic, 2003), p. 166.

67. Raymond E. Brown, *The Community of the Beloved Disciple* (New York: Paulist Press, 1979), p. 87.

the Christian movement, approving every major step taken."[68] In the Fourth Gospel, however, "the disciples closest to Jesus do not form any kind of hierarchy, nor are they given any particular office. As James Dunn points out, they are never called 'apostles' and only once 'the Twelve' (John 6:67)."[69] Instead, Jesus' followers are described in egalitarian terms: they are "those who believe" (17:2), "those who know the truth" (8:23), "children of God" (1:12; 11:52), "sheep" (John 10:1-18), "servants" (12:26; 13:16), "branches" of the vine, "friends" (15:13), and "those the Father gave Jesus out of the world" (17:6). The primary category of the Fourth Gospel is that of "disciple" — a picture of a fellowship of equals, with no hint of rank. D. Moody Smith suggests that

> because the Twelve are seldom mentioned and never named, because Peter seems to be put down in favor of the Beloved Disciple, because the importance of direct access of the believer to Jesus is emphasized, because the risen Christ seems to preside over his church through the Spirit-Paraclete; for all these reasons it is widely held that John represents a "low" ecclesiology or a view of church order in which ministerial office has not developed or has not been allowed to develop. Rather, every believer is related to Christ in the same way.[70]

There is one special category in the Johannine Gospel: that of the "Beloved Disciple." The Beloved Disciple is singled out by John to symbolize "the individual believer in the immediacy and closeness of his relationship with Jesus (13:23-25, 20:2-8)."[71] Here again we see the personalism of the Fourth Gospel at work: the Beloved Disciple reclines close to Jesus' breast at the Last Supper, and Jesus entrusts his own mother to him at the foot of the cross. The category of discipleship based on love makes all other hierarchical distinctions in the Johannine community relatively unimportant. At the Last Supper, even Peter, the head of the apostles, may not talk directly to Jesus but has to channel his question through the Beloved Disciple, who has special intimacy. Furthermore, the well-known Petrine presbyteral im-

---

68. Brown, *The Community of the Beloved Disciple*, p. 86.

69. Dunn, "John and the Synoptics as a Theological Question," p. 255.

70. D. Moody Smith, *Johannine Christianity: Essays on Its Setting, Sources, and Theology* (Columbia: University of South Carolina Press, 1984), p. 212.

71. Dunn, "John and the Synoptics as a Theological Question," p. 255.

age of the shepherd is introduced with the conditioning question, "Do you love me? (21:15-17)."[72] In his closeness to Jesus, the Beloved Disciple is the paradigmatic model for all future followers of Christ (cf. 17:20; 20:29). Indeed, Dwight Moody Smith suggests that this is the reason that he remains unnamed: "Any and all disciples of Jesus may become beloved disciples. Such disciples, whom Jesus loves, are the church."[73]

3. *The Prioritization of Christology.* The debate over sacraments in the Fourth Gospel is one of the most complicated and persistent in New Testament scholarship. Unlike the Synoptics, the Fourth Gospel offers no narrative about the Lord's Supper and no story of Jesus' baptism. Some exegetes have found Eucharistic associations in the wine at Cana, the meals of bread and fish, and the figure of the vine and branches, while others stress that bread and wine are never found *together* in these examples.[74] This ambiguity is difficult to resolve, especially since it seems that most interpreters find their own ecclesial commitments when they gaze into the deep well of the Fourth Gospel. Perhaps Robert Kysar is right to assert that "no amount of research or study will (or even should) finally resolve the [Johannine sacramental] ambiguity."[75] Because both sacramental and nonsacramental interpretations of Johannine passages have a degree of truth, different reading communities are justified in bringing their differing interpretations to the texts.[76]

---

72. Brown, *The Community of the Beloved Disciple*, p. 87.

73. D. Moody Smith, *The Theology of the Gospel of John* (New York: Cambridge University Press, 1995), p. 154.

74. See Craig R. Koester, *Symbolism in the Fourth Gospel: Meaning, Mystery, Community* (Minneapolis: Fortress Press, 2003), 302: "The first Cana miracle entails turning water into wine, but the passage makes no mention of bread; Jesus feeds the five thousand with bread and fish, but not wine; and the image of the vine focuses on fruit bearing rather than eating or drinking."

75. Robert Kysar, *Voyages with John: Charting the Fourth Gospel* (Waco: Baylor University Press, 2005), p. 249.

76. Both sacramental and nonsacramental interpretations were deemed viable at the Council of Trent, and forms of the nonsacramental view are attested from the second century onward in the writings of Clement of Alexandria (d. ca. 215), Origen (d. 254), Eusebius (d. 340), and others. This was the primary position of Augustine (d. 430) and the one considered least problematic by Thomas Aquinas (d. 1274). It was also followed in various ways by Desiderius Erasmus (d. 1536), Martin Luther (d. 1546), John Calvin (d. 1564), and others. See Koester, *Symbolism in the Fourth Gospel*, pp. 304-5.

However, in carving out a space for both sacramental and nonsacramental positions, one must not conflate the situation of the first-century church with Reformation debates. Although "sacramental piety" may have been a problem in the post-Reformation era, applying this criticism to the historical Johannine situation seems forced.[77] With this caution in mind, Paul Anderson suggests that the ambiguity surrounding sacraments in the Fourth Gospel

> may reflect an ideological disagreement between the centripetal ways late first-century leaders sought to counteract the centrifugal tendencies of the sub-apostolic era. An acute emphasis on cultic ritual involvement was one of these, and while it is anachronistic to assume the evangelist was an "anti-sacramentalist," he may indeed have objected to institutionalizing attempts to centralize the church. He apparently disagreed with the rise of ordinance motifs and understood the unifying power of faith in Jesus Christ to be better expressed in relational and familial ways than ritual ones.[78]

There is little reason to doubt that Johannine Christians celebrated the Eucharist: indeed, the fact that John makes use of the words of institution in 6:51c might testify to this practice. Furthermore, the absence of any actual polemic against baptism or the celebration of communion should caution us against reading John as an "anti-sacramentalist." Instead, the silences surrounding the rites themselves should best be understood "as a signal of John's fundamental preoccupation with the greater 'sacrament,' the Word made flesh, the revelation of God and the access to the Father made present and visible in the incarnation of Jesus."[79] Put differently, "John betrays no interest in church practices or structures in themselves; he tacitly presupposes them and concentrates on the person of Christ as their basis."[80] Turning the Johannine material into a discussion about the Eucharistic elements risks missing the Christological imperative of the text:

---

77. Paul N. Anderson, *The Christology of the Fourth Gospel: Its Unity and Disunity in the Light of John 6* (Tübingen: J. C. B. Mohr, 1996), p. 115.

78. Anderson, *The Christology of the Fourth Gospel*, p. 135.

79. David A. DeSilva, *An Introduction to the New Testament* (Downers Grove, Ill.: InterVarsity Press, 2004), p. 429.

80. Martinus J. J. Menken, "John 6:51c-58: Eucharist or Christology?," in *Critical Readings of John 6* (Leiden: E. J. Brill, 1997), p. 202.

What this Gospel is interested in from first to last is the one person that all the Gospel signs and sayings point to — Jesus Christ. It does not pause more than briefly to reflect on a sign's qualities, characteristics, or elements as if it were an object that is intrinsically interesting, but focuses like a laser on the thing to which the sign points.[81]

In an interesting parallel, evangelical theologian Donald Bloesch expresses a similar concern about *Baptism, Eucharist, and Ministry.* Bloesch cautions, "BEM rightly affirms the real presence of Christ in the Eucharist, but it needs to warn against focusing on the outward signs rather than on the transcendent reality to which the signs point."[82]

If anything can be read between the lines from an examination of the Fourth Gospel, it is this: "the Johannine community was neither a particularly sacramental nor antisacramental group. . . . It was interested in focusing on christological, not ecclesiological or sacramental matters."[83] Here again for John, what is truly essential is the living presence of Jesus in the Christian through the Paraclete: no institution or structure can substitute for that.[84] Herein lies the evangelical concern. As Timothy George explains, defining the church as sacrament "obscures the sole sufficiency and sovereignty of Jesus Christ, who remains supremely free and does not surrender his royal prerogative even to the community that bears his name, nor to the signs and seals with which he blesses, nourishes, and sanctifies his Body."[85] George cites John 3:8 in support of the fact that the church and its sacraments are never "eminent subjects of causality." Christ "neither shares his glory nor gives his lordship to anyone else, not even to the church. The wind of the Spirit blows wherever it pleases."[86]

81. Ben Witherington, *John's Wisdom: A Commentary on the Fourth Gospel* (Louisville: Westminster John Knox Press, 1995), p. 96.

82. Donald G. Bloesch, *The Church: Sacraments, Worship, Ministry, Mission* (Downers Grove, Ill.: InterVarsity Press, 2002), p. 177.

83. Witherington, *John's Wisdom,* pp. 96-97.

84. Brown, *The Community of the Beloved Disciple,* p. 88.

85. Timothy George, "The Sacramentality of the Church: An Evangelical Baptist Perspective," *Pro Ecclesia* 12, no. 3 (2003): 320.

86. George, "The Sacramentality of the Church," p. 317.

Conclusion

The goal of this chapter has been to move beyond labels of "catholic exceptions" and "gnostic tendencies" to show that nonsacramental Christianity
is one faithful way of embodying the shared confession of faith. My hope is
that the discipline of liturgical studies is wide enough to embrace "both-and"
without mandating "either-or." David Wright makes this point clear when he
observes that every Christian operates with a body of functional theology
that has strengths and weaknesses, one-sided preoccupations, and surprising
silences and lacunae. He continues:

> When I hear or read others expounding a theme or an emphasis that have
> no place in my working theology, more often than not I instinctively rec-
> ognize their truthfulness and importance. Yet rarely do such experiences
> lead to my rejigging my functional theology to incorporate what I have
> neglected or never known of. Some marginal adjustments may occur,
> but for the most part I am happy to let others be the guardians of, say,
> the eucharistic dimension of the church's being or the significance of the
> inclusion or exclusion of *Filioque*.[87]

Wright acknowledges the need for humility on this side of the eschaton:
communities and communions are diverse, and our limitations as human
beings include time, space, economic status, intellect, and industry. He
concludes, "a certain modesty is appropriate . . . especially when those with
whom we do not see eye-to-eye share the same allegiance to Scripture."[88]

It is in precisely this spirit of humility that I offer my reading of John.
If the one event of Jesus requires four Gospels, and if the single confession
of faith requires a diversity of liturgical expressions, then it is reasonable
to claim that the exegesis of the one Bible requires numerous interpreters.
Whereas I detect clear parallels between Johannine and Free Church ecclesiology, Catholic and Orthodox biblical scholars have recommended the

87. David F. Wright, "Scripture and Evangelical Diversity with Special Reference to the
Baptismal Divide," in *A Pathway into the Holy Scripture*, ed. Philip E. Satterthwaite and David F.
Wright (Grand Rapids: Wm. B. Eerdmans, 1994), p. 273.

88. Wright, "Scripture and Evangelical Diversity with Special Reference to the Baptismal
Divide," p. 273.

Johannine literature to their liturgical traditions as the most sacramental of the New Testament. Similarly, it is entirely appropriate for Lathrop to discover in John a continuation of the *ordo* he sees rooted in the Synoptics. No one ecclesial tradition can claim the definitive interpretation of this book. In fact, this is precisely the point. Kevin Vanhoozer explains that "just as many members make up one body, so many readings make up the single correct interpretation."[89]

Two extremes must be avoided. On the one hand, the Fourth Gospel must not become the paradigm to which the Synoptics must conform. An example of this approach is found in Robert Gundry's work, *Jesus the Word according to John the Sectarian: A Paleofundamentalist Manifesto for Contemporary Evangelicalism, Especially Its Elites, in North America*. Gundry worries that a healthy Johannine "sense of embattlement with the world is rapidly evaporating among many evangelicals, especially 'evangelical elites,' among them those who belong to 'the knowledge industry.'"[90] Gundry singles out liturgy and sacrament for special treatment by arguing many of the points made above:

> The stress of John the sectarian on verbal communication by Jesus the Word leads him to depress sacrament and liturgy. The baptism of Jesus goes unmentioned. His baptism of others is introduced only to provide an occasion for John the Baptist's testimony to Jesus' superiority as the one who "speaks the words of God". . . . Nor does John's version of the Great Commission (20:21) contain a command to carry on the practice of baptism. . . . And despite John's devotion of several chapters to the Last Supper, he omits the Institution of the Lord's Supper and transmutes the Words of Institution into metaphors for the life- and Spirit-giving benefit of believing Jesus' words (6:52).

On the basis of this exegesis, Gundry concludes that it is time for "John's anti- or at least un-sacramentalism to halt [the evangelical] drift into the

---

89. Kevin Vanhoozer, *Is There a Meaning in This Text? The Bible, the Reader, and the Morality of Literary Knowledge* (Grand Rapids: Zondervan, 1998), p. 420.

90. Robert H. Gundry, *Jesus the Word according to John the Sectarian: A Paleofundamentalist Manifesto for Contemporary Evangelicalism, Especially Its Elites, in North America* (Grand Rapids: Wm B. Eerdmans, 2002), p. 73.

sacramentalism that characterizes institutional churches and into the liturgies that frame such sacramentalism."[91] The problem with this approach, as Mark Noll notes, is that "Gundry hangs the lessons he draws from John's Gospel on his interpretation of John's Gospel alone, not on how his interpretation of that one Gospel may be brought together with interpretation of the other Gospels, the rest of the New Testament, or the rest of Scripture as a whole."[92]

On the other hand, the unified witness of the Synoptic Gospels must not be allowed to overpower the distinctive contributions of John. Raymond Brown suggests that the book of John offers other churches a significant liturgical corrective: "It can remind the mainline churches, as it did Christians in the first century, that an individual relationship with Jesus is a necessary component of sound ecclesiology."[93] Brown continues:

> In addition to providing doctrine and pastoral care, liturgy and sacraments, and a supportive sense of belonging to a caring community, a church must bring people into some personal contact with Jesus so that they can experience in their own way what made people follow him in the first place. . . . That Christ willed or founded the church may be adequate theology for some; but an abstraction, focused on the past, will not be enough to keep others loyal to a church unless they encounter Jesus there.[94]

Certainly there are significant ecclesiological differences between Frontier-*ordo* churches and ecumenical-*ordo* churches that we should not gloss over. The problems that Charles Finney bequeathed the American church in general and evangelicalism in particular are real and unresolved: they deserve to be named and engaged by scholars from across denominational traditions. However, scholars must be careful of either-or dichotomies that pit one liturgical tradition against another by using one section of Scripture against another. Mark Noll offers a timely caution on this point: "While it is healthy to see the mixed messages in Scripture (just so long as they are actually

91. Gundry, *Jesus the Word according to John the Sectarian*, pp. 75-76, p. 91.

92. Mark Noll, "Comment on Robert Gundry," *Evangelical Studies Bulletin* 19, no. 1 (Spring 2002): 4.

93. Brown, *The Churches the Apostles Left Behind*, pp. 95-96.

94. Brown, *The Churches the Apostles Left Behind*, p. 97.

there), it cannot be intellectually or spiritually helpful to see these messages as incoherent or fully contradictory."[95]

The lesson of twentieth-century hermeneutics is that readings and interpretations of texts are never neutral or exhaustive. Readers can no more step out of our place, time, culture, and social situation than escape our human finitude. For this reason, Vanhoozer is entirely right to assert that it would "be most regrettable if the church everywhere and at all times had to conform to, say, 1970s North American Evangelicalism. Evangelicalism in any decade provides only a few limited snapshots of what the Christian faith looks like when incarnated in a specific place and period."[96] However, it would be equally regrettable if ecumenical theologians *neglected* the gifts that North American evangelicalism of the 1970s (or any decade) brings to the liturgical table. The unity of the Spirit is "an ethical unity — a unity of love — that welcomes legitimate differences without seeking to reduce them to uniformity."[97]

This insight leads to a concluding confluence of insights from biblical (Kevin Vanhoozer), systematic (Miroslav Volf), and liturgical (Aidan Kavanagh) theologians. In his writings on biblical hermeneutics, Vanhoozer affirms a "Pentecostal plurality," which "maintains that the one true interpretation is best approximated by a diversity of particular methods and contexts of reading."[98] Volf makes a similar point when he cites the miracle at Pentecost as a "primal catholic event." The Spirit of God removed "the communication breach caused by the language confusion of the Tower of Babel." However, it is significant that Pentecost was not simply "Babel in reverse." The Christians of Acts 2 did not all speak *one* language — a move that Volf suggests "would represent an ill-fated return to the uniformity of Babel." Instead, the communication at Pentecost came about "through the speaking of *different* languages. The eschatological catholicity of the people of God is thereby reflected in a broken fashion in history.[99]

The diversity of liturgical systems is in many ways analogous to the

95. Noll, "Comment on Robert Gundry," pp. 4-5.
96. Kevin J. Vanhoozer, *The Drama of Doctrine: A Canonical-Linguistic Approach to Christian Theology* (Louisville: Westminster John Knox Press, 2005), p. 27.
97. Vanhoozer, *Is There a Meaning in This Text?*, p. 421.
98. Vanhoozer, *Is There a Meaning in This Text?*, p. 419.
99. Volf, *After Our Likeness*, p. 268.

diversity of human languages. As Kavanagh notes, "Even an untrained observer can tell the obvious differences between French and English, between a Byzantine Divine Liturgy and a Methodist Covenant Service."[100] Worshipping traditions no more speak one liturgical language than do the first Christians at Pentecost, and the reality of this diversity is the reason that it is problematic to talk about either "language" or "liturgy" in a general way. Both words are convenient abstractions, "capable of obscuring real differences by the splendor of sameness."[101]

This is not to say that diverse liturgical patterns have nothing in common. Kavanagh detects an elusive similarity "in baroque pontifical Masses and in helter-skelter baptisms in basements," in "St. Mary Major on Good Friday and in a small oratory in Indiana on a ferial Wednesday," "during the reading of the martyrology at prime in a monastery and during Benediction of the Blessed Sacrament on a hillside in Tennessee."[102] But Kavanagh urges scholars to proceed with caution: comparative methodology must not be allowed to dissolve into cheap sentimentality. In order to get beneath a liturgy's surface structure, "one must learn new vocabulary, alien grammar, [and] different syntax," and it is only through "great discipline" and "years of constant effort" that scholars can begin to discover deep commonality across liturgical systems.[103] Kavanagh rightly notes, "Liturgy, like language, is not always logical, and one who begins to learn one language by studying language in general begins badly."[104]

The next chapter in this book is an exercise in Kavanagh's mandate for specificity. For my second case study, I traveled to West Shore Evangelical Free Church in Mechanicsburg, Pennsylvania. Here I discovered that if scholars move beyond the surface structure of the Frontier *ordo,* they will discover deep theological commonality between evangelical and liturgical worship traditions.

100. Kavanagh, *On Liturgical Theology,* p. 80.
101. Kavanagh, *On Liturgical Theology,* p. 79.
102. Kavanagh, *On Liturgical Theology,* p. 77.
103. Kavanagh, *On Liturgical Theology,* p. 80.
104. Kavanagh, *On Liturgical Theology,* p. 79.

CHAPTER FIVE

Case Study 2:
West Shore Evangelical Free Church

> *I think that when we gather for worship at West Shore, God reveals himself in a unique way in the context of the event. Where two or three are gathered on any given Sunday, there God will be in our midst in a new and fresh way. Perhaps the reason we don't follow an Episcopal or Presbyterian or any other denominational liturgy is because we're afraid it will get in the way of the ability of God's Spirit.*

Doug, worship leader, West Shore Evangelical Free Church

Worship at West Shore: A Snapshot

It is the first Sunday in February, shortly before nine A.M., and the sanctuary of West Shore Evangelical Free Church (WSEFC) in Mechanicsburg, Pennsylvania, is slowly coming to life. At the front of the room on the right sits a powerful church organ; on the platform stage behind it stands a grand piano, a full drum set behind a plastic sound barrier, and an array of guitars, monitors, and microphones. A wooden cross, easily ten feet in size and backlit in soft colors, hangs above the platform. It is clearly visible from all points in the sanctuary, as are the two large projection screens hanging to its far left and far right. These screens display announcements before the service begins; later on, they will be the congregation's reference point for responsive readings, Scripture texts, and song lyrics. Many of those gathering juggle coffee cups, diaper bags, and Bibles simultaneously. Hugs are exchanged; news is swapped; babies are bounced and admired. Some families turn and mount the steps at the rear of the sanctuary, eventually settling into graduated rows of seating behind a large soundboard. Others remain on the flat carpeting and claim a chair in one of the rows facing the platform.

As the organ prelude fades away, an associate pastor steps up to the microphone. A series of announcements follows, after which the congregation is invited to stand and greet one another. "Good mornings," grins, and handshakes are passed down the rows. Many of the people seated near me know my academic background; some wink and initiate a more formal liturgical greeting ("The peace of Christ be with you," "The peace of the Lord be with you") when we make eye contact. A few minutes pass, and the morning worship leader takes her place at the front of the platform. She signals the organist, and the opening chords of "Come, Christians, Join to Sing" fill the sanctuary. The congregation joins in immediately, and heartily, singing three stanzas with gusto. The hymn swells to its conclusion, and after a suspended pause, the guitars and percussion establish a new rhythm. Upon hearing a short introduction, the congregation recognizes the chorus. "We have come to a throne of grace,/where our mighty Savior/perfects our praise," they sing. "You're the King of grace unending,/and we rest in your unfailing love."[1] The chorus repeats for several minutes before slowing to a conclusion. The congregation then participates responsively in a composite Scripture reading:

> Leader: He is the image of the invisible God, the firstborn over all creation.
>
> **All: For by him all things were created: things in heaven and on earth, visible and invisible, whether thrones or powers or rulers or authorities; all things were created by him and for him.**
>
> Leader: He is before all things, and in him all things hold together.
>
> **All: And he is the head of the body, the church; he is the beginning and the firstborn from among the dead, so that in everything he might have the supremacy.**
>
> Leader: God was pleased to have all his fullness dwell in him, and through him to reconcile to himself all things, whether things on

---

1. Mark Altrogge, "King of Grace" (copyright 2000 by Sovereign Grace Music).

earth or things in heaven, by making peace through his blood, shed
on the cross.

Leader: Therefore God exalted him to the highest place and gave him
the name that is above every name,

**All: that at the name of Jesus every knee should bow, in heaven and
on earth and under the earth, and every tongue confess that Jesus
Christ is Lord, to the glory of God the Father.**

As the congregation settles into their seats, the pianist begins the introduction of the next chorus, "Your Name." Its lyrics dovetail well with
the verses from Philippians: "Your name, higher than them all;/Holy One
of God, the Lord of lords./Your name, your name." The atmosphere in the
sanctuary has shifted from exultant to contemplative as the congregation
sings, "All nations bow, their kingdoms fall;/every king and priest, every
prince and lord,/falling on their knees will acknowledge you./We will lift
our voice in praise/and honor your name."[2]

Phil, the senior pastor, moves to the front of the room and reads from
Revelation 1:12-20. At the conclusion of the Scripture reading, he offers an
extemporaneous prayer:

Lord Jesus, you are the everlasting God: the one who spoke the worlds into
existence at the beginning of time. You are the one who holds everything
together by your mighty word. And you are the one who left his throne
in glory and entered into our human flesh and bone. You are the one
who died our death on the cross. You are the one that descended into the
darker regions and there battled the very forces of sin and death. You are
the one that was raised victorious from the dead and are now seated at the
right hand of God the Father Almighty. You are the one who, if we could
see you now, is shining — your face blazing like the sun in all its glory. You
are the one around whom angels continue to sing, "Glory, glory!" Lord
Jesus, forgive us. Forgive us for not giving you your rightful place in our
hearts. Forgive us for disobeying the King of the Universe. Forgive us for
not even holding you in our minds and hearts, for being distracted and
drawn by such lesser glories. Lord Jesus, don't just forgive us. Send your

2. Andy Bromley, "Your Name" (copyright 1998 by Thankyou Music).

Spirit. Send your Spirit in power to set us free from the things that draw us away from you; set us free from the things that cloud our minds and that cloud our minds' eyes. Set us free to see who you are, and what you have done, and what you have called us to be. Fill us with a vision of your glory, for your sake, and for the sake of those who do not yet know you. In your strong name we pray, Amen.

Ushers come forward to receive the offering, while the congregation sings a Trinitarian song of praise: "Wonderful, merciful Savior;/Precious Redeemer and Friend./Who would have thought that a Lamb/could rescue the souls of men?/Counselor, Comforter, Keeper:/Spirit we long to embrace./You offer hope when our hearts have/hopelessly lost the way./Almighty, infinite Father,/faithfully loving Your own./Here in our weakness You find us/falling before Your throne."[3]

The sermon is from Colossians 1, and Phil wastes no time getting to the heart of the matter: "He is the image of the invisible God." By "he," Phil clarifies, Paul means the pre-existent, eternal Son of the eternal God — Jesus before and after his birth. The Apostle John calls this pre-existent Jesus *the Word*. The pre-incarnate Christ has the position of firstborn pre-eminence over all creation, because he is its creator. Phil proceeds to outline the familiar story. Before time and the foundation of the world, God has enjoyed the glory and goodness of his own being, living as Father, Son, and Holy Spirit with indescribable joy and pleasure. At some point, which we call "the beginning," God decided to create beings that were other than himself and to give those beings the privilege of experiencing some measure of his goodness, beauty, and truth. Humans turned away from God, creating wars, oppression, injustice, hatred, strife, and the disintegration of the human soul. Christ became a human being who would do what no human being had ever done — he would live a life of complete and perfect union with the Father. He would die on the cross for the sins of the world and would rise from the dead to defeat the power of sin and death. God would send his Spirit upon his people and begin to transform them, giving them a new heart and enabling them to live a new life and create a new kind of history. Jesus is not

3. Eric Wyse and Dawn Rodgers, "Wonderful, Merciful Savior" (copyright 1989 by Word Music).

only the head, the firstborn, of creation, but also the beginning of a whole new creation.

After his exegesis, Phil challenges the congregation with a series of questions. "How big is your picture of Jesus? Is Jesus like a religious rabbit's foot you carry around in your pocket and rub with a prayer every once in a while for good luck? Or do you think of the resurrected Jesus Christ in the book of Revelation, standing with his face shining like the sun? Do you think of the eternal Word who spoke the worlds into existence and who holds them together by his power?" This leads to another question: "How big is your picture of salvation? When you think of the gospel, do you think of the beginning of the four spiritual laws — that God loves you and has a wonderful plan for your life? Or do you think of the 'all things' of Colossians 1:20? It was not just for you and me that Jesus died," Phil reiterates. "Salvation is cosmic. It involves the total transformation of all created reality, and is nothing short of the reconciliation of all things to God — the accomplishment of his eternal purpose to bring everything together to its appointed end in Jesus. Did you think it was just praying a prayer to get a ticket into heaven?" Finally, Phil asks the congregation, "How big is your life? Do you realize that God has called you to be the body of Christ — the visible manifestation of Christ's invisible presence in the world — his hands, feet, eyes, and voice, if you will? God has called you to be the place where his Holy Spirit dwells. He has given us the opportunity to join his mission to transform created reality through the person of his Son — the purpose he has been accomplishing from before the beginning of time."

The congregation responds with four stanzas of "When I Survey the Wondrous Cross." The final verse feels like an especially appropriate response to the cosmic nature of salvation: "Were the whole realm of nature mine,/ That were a present far too small;/Love so amazing, so divine,/Demands my soul, my life, my all." As the final notes of the piano and organ recede, Phil extends his hand in a blessing: "May Jesus be the center of our lives so that the world may know that he is the center of human history. Go in peace."

Historical and Demographical Information

West Shore is a 110,000-square-foot, $30-million facility that sits on 92 acres and serves between 2,500 and 2,750 people on any given Sunday. At the be-

ginning of my three-month study, forty employees and fourteen staff members gathered around the ministerial table. The church operates on a four- $40 million
million-dollar budget, $300,000 to $500,000 of which represents its annual
missions commitment. Globally, it sustains partnerships with churches in
Bosnia and Cambodia and with a theological college in Zimbabwe. Locally, it
offers (among other things) a professional counseling ministry and church-
wide blood-pressure screenings. A monthly Saturday-morning "Caring
Closet" provides free clothing, shoes, and household items to anyone in the
community in need. As Phil explained to me, "WSEFC is the size of thirty
average churches in America. It is organizationally challenging and complex,
and it takes a lot of energy just to sustain that reality."

When Phil accepted the call to this pastorate sixteen years ago, he expressed a desire to remain at the church for twenty to twenty-five years. "I
wanted the privilege of performing weddings for the children I dedicated,"
he once explained to me. "I grew up in that kind of a church, and I think it
makes ministry qualitatively different." Phil is a gifted pastor with a passion
for biblical exegesis. He is also a man of formidable intellect. Phil earned
his doctorate in theology from Cambridge University, where he cultivated
his affinity for the work of Karl Barth. His personal library contains over
four thousand volumes; academic references to "Polanyian epistemology,"
"Ockham's razor," and "second naïveté" pepper my transcripts of our conversations together.

The congregation is primarily white, suburban, and middle class — a
reflection of the socioeconomic demographic within a ten-mile radius of
the church. The church is part of the Evangelical Free Church of America,
an association of some 1,500 autonomous and interdependent churches and
church plants. However, most of the people who attend this church have not
grown up in the denomination. (One member remarked to me, "We don't
have people who are lifelong, Evangelical Free Church people here. A lot of
people don't really know what Evangelical Free is. I mean, I don't, and I've
even looked into it and had a class and stuff.")

Phil concurs: "People from across a wide spectrum are coming together
in a church like ours." He suggests why: "People in the mainline are frustrated over the theological drift and the lack of evangelical fervor. It's not just
the fact that we hold to a more 'conservative' or 'traditional' theology. It's also
because there's a sense of energy, a sense of belief in the experienced pres

why pp attend

ence of God *this* Sunday, *this* week in my life." He adds, "I also have people coming up to me from independent fundamentalist churches and saying, 'This is a breath of fresh air. There's not a legalism here; there's freedom to disagree on nonessential matters.' We're the church where the disgruntled and hurt fundamentalists come, and we're the church where the disillusioned mainline comes."

The church is two stories high, has multiple points of entry (there is no singular, easily identifiable front door), and is surrounded by parking lots. Lush, field-like lawns encompass the parking lots, and there is a beautiful view from almost every window of the building. This green space was intentionally designed to maintain the farming/residential feel of the adjacent neighborhood. Inside the church, museum-quality dioramas of jungle animals interwoven with verses about creation enliven the walls of the children's ministry wing. Students are assigned by ages to animal-themed classrooms: the "Elephants and Ostriches," for example, or the "Aardvarks and Walruses." In these rooms, two- and three-year-olds learn about the life of Jesus; four-year-olds participate in an overview of the Old Testament; five-year-olds explore the New Testament; and so on. On Sundays and Wednesdays, noisy junior and senior high-school students cluster in the Youth Café — a 1950s-styled diner equipped with booths, a soda fountain, a foosball table, an air-hockey table, and a pool table. Fellowship groups for adults abound: some are intentionally intergenerational; others are organized around a particular stage of life.

Many members of the congregation would identify the "A-Team" — the church's ministry to individuals with cognitive disabilities — as the crown jewel of West Shore's fellowship groups. This ministry holds a special place in the congregation's heart. The A-Team's founding members named themselves after a popular 1980s television show as a reflection of their tenacity and willingness to face challenges. Today, the group boasts about fifty members. They meet together every Sunday morning for worship and Bible study, in classes grouped by approximate levels of cognitive understanding, social skills, and independence. The A-team is not simply a Sunday school class but also actively ministers in the life of the wider church. The team presents an annual Christmas play for the congregation and the wider community and has helped serve monthly communion nearly ninety times. Together, the group offers regular financial and prayer support to the children it sponsors in the Dominican Republic, and it has sent smaller groups of its members overseas. The team's travels have taken them to Puerto Rico, London, and twice to Africa, where volunteers served at a hospital for disabled children in Kijabe.

Boys and girls clubs stream in and out of the church on weeknights. Women's, men's, and couples' Bible studies are available multiple weekday afternoons and evenings. Choir members trickle through the building for rehearsal; youth square off against one another in friendly basketball competitions hosted at the church's gym. Frazzled parents trail energetic children into the library to check out Bible storybooks and family-friendly DVDs. Information kiosks are located on upper and lower levels of the church's lobbies: here anyone can seek answers to general questions, or request a building map, a list of current fellowship groups, information about upcoming ministry events, and offering envelopes. Books, sermon series, CDs, and devotional aids are sold in the church's small bookstore; coffee, tea, and hot chocolate are made available to the congregation every Sunday morning.

The hustle and bustle is such that some of the church's long-standing members have dubbed the building "our Mega-gelical Freeplex" — an affectionate scrambling of the phrase "evangelical megaplex." One congregation member noted that "a massive amount of people" attend the church but cheerfully added, "Big churches only mean more brothers and sisters." Comments like these might seem glib at best, or triumphalistic at worst. However, after spending only a short time with the congregation, I was left with a different impression. The church's ability to laugh about its size is genuine, but also self-conscious. WSEFC is a church of humble beginnings, and, despite the bells and whistles of its new building, it is used to thinking of itself as an average-sized, local congregation.

The church's history began in 1975, when forty-five men and women gathered for worship in classroom space borrowed from a nearby college, and later in sacred space borrowed from a local Jewish synagogue. Five years later, the fledgling church constructed its own new building, where it remained for twenty-four years. This building underwent a series of renovations to accommodate the congregation's steady growth, including the addition of a Christian education wing in the late 1980s and a youth ministry center in 2001. When the church moved out of its first building and into its current location in 2005, its facilities nearly tripled in size: the church swelled from 40,000 square feet in the old building to 110,000 square feet in the new. In the original building, 550 chairs were squeezed into a tightly packed sanctuary each Sunday for worship. The new sanctuary's stadium seating comfortably accommodates 1,450.

On one level, the church's self-consciousness about its new physical magnitude is emotional. A congregation that was used to bumping elbows in the hall, squeezing tightly together in cramped worship spaces, and rolling its collective eyes at logjams in the narthex between services now has room to move about freely. But with this gain comes an unexpected sense of loss. Although no one I talked to expressed a desire to return to the cramped older building — indeed, most feel very blessed to have a larger sanctuary, more classroom space, and other such amenities — many members miss the solidarity and camaraderie that came from "making do" under less-than-ideal circumstances.

But there is another subtle, spiritual component to the church's self-consciousness. Two years after moving into its new facility, Phil preached a series of sermons in conversation with the book *unChristian* by David Kinnaman and Gabe Lyons. The premise of the book is simple and disturbing: something has gone terribly wrong with modern Christianity. The book's three-year study of individuals between the ages of 19 and 35 — adults who had spent their formative childhood and adolescent years inside the church — overwhelmingly indicated that they now perceived Christians to be judgmental, antihomosexual, hypocritical, too political, and sheltered. *unChristian* created a shock wave not only in the WSEFC congregation but also in the evangelical world at large. Phil offers an apt summary:

> Most young adults who look at American Christianity are not impressed. They look at the music and say, "They're trying to be contemporary, but this is kind of hokey." They have a bias against anything that looks pre-sentational and slick, anything that's too "programmed." They look at the church and say, "What I mostly see are people who are interested in being successful, having enough money, and living the American dream, all the while baptizing their American dream in Christian language." We are considered "unChristian" by the world around us, and most of those people have spent quite a bit of time in church. We ought to be big enough

to own their criticisms, to say, "You're right." We have to admit it, address it, confess it, and work against it.

On the whole, it seems that the congregation shares their pastor's convictions but is unsure how to respond. One member confessed, "I feel a struggle right now, both personally and in our church community, about how to reach churchgoers of both older generations and the twenty/thirty-something generation. WSEFC has talked a lot about the problem, but I don't think we have done enough to address the issue concretely."

WSEFC wrestles with these issues regularly and intensely. As mentioned above, the congregation is well aware that a younger generation — disillusioned by mall-like environments, music that tries too hard to be "contemporary," "slick" ministries, and a general "baptizing of the American dream in Christian language" — is leaving evangelicalism in unprecedented numbers. The issue is ecclesiological, and Phil addressed it repeatedly in sermons during my study. Phil once asked the congregation,

> What do you want people to say when they look at our church? Do you want them to say, "Wow! Look at that incredible building. Wow! Check out their children's ministry, their youth ministry, their music!" Or do you want them to say, "You know, there is something about the *people* in that church — the quality of their lives, the depth of their relationships, the way they seem to know God. I have to hear more about this Jesus they keep talking about."

In another sermon, Phil made the following point:

> Modern church work, in a big church like ours, sometimes feels like the work of producing programs for religious consumers. Worship programs for religious spectators sitting in a Sunday-morning auditorium. Sermons can become commodities that people consume and criticize. I mean, you can even buy them on a CD. Children's ministries can become producers of sports programs and education programs and music programs; and youth ministry can slide into entertainment. Before you know it, pastors have become religious shopkeepers; the best pastors are the ones who can build and supply the best religious stores — the Walmarts of the religious

world. *But church work is about people.* It's about participating with God in the work of transforming people's lives — helping each become more like Jesus; helping each other bring the life and love of God to the people in this world.

In yet another sermon, Phil explained what it means to be the church:

> Do you know what the church is? The church is not this building. The church isn't even the sum total of all the programs of ministry that go on in this building — the children's ministry, the youth ministry, the worship ministry, the preaching ministry. The church is not a place you go to or programs that you participate in. It's not something that you invite someone to come to so they can meet God. *The church, biblically, is you.* It's the people of God, filled with the Spirit of God, living the life of God in the world. Or as we sometimes say in this church, being like and becoming like Jesus.

Theological Analysis

"Becoming Like Jesus: Head, Heart, Hands, Knees, Feet." Even with its emphasis on reaching the next generation, it would be wrong to label WSEFC a "seeker-driven" church. In his article "Lex Agendi, Lex Orandi," Lester Ruth suggests that seeker services invert the paradigm established by the Constitution on the Sacred Liturgy: "the liturgy is the summit toward which the activity of the Church is directed; at the same time it is also the fount from which all her power flows." Ruth suggests that churches which have adopted seeker services have also created a new role for the liturgy: evangelism is now *the* defining activity of the church, and liturgy is "a subservient tool to be shaped and pragmatically used for this end."[4]

In my conversations with Phil, a different picture emerged. Almost ten years ago, the senior pastor and elder board got together in a series of meetings to evaluate the church's mission statement. In keeping with Ruth's

---

4. Lester Ruth, "Lex Agendi, Lex Orandi: Toward an Understanding of Seeker Services as a New Kind of Liturgy," *Worship* 70, no. 5 (1996): 402.

theory, many on the elder board and in the congregation wanted the classic evangelical emphases of "fulfilling the Great Commission" and "reaching the lost" to define the summit of their church's activity. However, Phil was uneasy with singling out any one activity — either worship or evangelism — as "the" source and summit of the church. As he explained to me, "I found it theologically objectionable to try to elevate worship over the ministry of the Word, or worship and Word over community or the communion of saints, or any of those over the mission of God and reaching the lost."

As a corrective, Phil turned to Scripture and identified six "life-giving" ecclesial practices of equal importance, with no one practice assuming dominance over any of the others. These practices include "learning and being transformed by the Word, worshipping, being in community, using our gifts in service, engaging in prayer, and going out on mission." In the years that followed, WSEFC experimented with a series of analogies that might best capture these practices in narrative form. They described their congregation as (1) a lighthouse for biblical proclamation, (2) a sanctuary for spiritual worship, (3) a home for caring community, (4) a training center for maturing disciples, (5) a house of prayer, and (6) a launching pad for worldwide mission. The church drew up a brochure explaining all six components, which it circulated widely at newcomers' breakfasts. Elders led in-depth discussions of the imagery in membership classes. Over the course of five years, Phil preached two series of sermons based on the phrases and Scripture allusions contained in the brochure.

But the imagery was complicated and didn't stick in the congregation's collective memory. So instead of a "sanctuary" and a "lighthouse," Phil began to speak about the church's "head" — faces lifted up in worship, and minds transformed by the Word of God. Rather than "home," the church reflected on its "heart" — a community where growing Christians experience and share God's love together. "Hands" replaced "training center" for the church's image of service, ministry, and love in action. "Knees" became the preferred language for describing the church as a house of prayer. Finally, "feet" supplanted "launching pad" as the metaphor for following Christ into the world. This revised, more integrated statement of the church's mission was introduced to the congregation in a series of sermons ten years ago; it continues to hold their theological imagination today. *"Becoming like Jesus: head, heart, hands, knees, and feet"* is now the church's motto. It appears on the church's web site and in its printed literature, and it was recited by the congregation in unison on the very first Sunday of my study. It is a metaphor that the smallest child can understand, that no adult has outgrown, and that the members of the A-Team have happily embraced.

Although the picture is simple, Phil stresses to the congregation that its underlying theology is richly Trinitarian. It begins with the Father, who elects and wills creatures for fellowship. Phil suggests that there are many places in the New Testament that illustrate this truth (Philippians 2, Ephesians 1, Colossians 3, Hebrews 12, etc.), but the passage that recurs most regularly in his discussions of the subject is Romans 8:29: "For those God foreknew, he also predestined to be conformed to the likeness of his Son, that he might be the firstborn among many brothers" (NIV). This means, Phil stresses, that God's commitment to humanity "stretches from before the beginning of time when God foreknew us, when he set his eyes upon us before the foundation of the world," and stretches "all the way to the end of time when we will be glorified." The Father's election can be established only through the Son, who justifies us and declares us righteous through his work on the cross. In Phil's summary, "becoming like Jesus is the good that God is working in our lives and is working in all of history to accomplish."

Of course, in an importance sense, "becoming like Jesus" is an impossible calling. Phil made this point clear in the sermon where he introduced the body analogy to the congregation. "Strictly speaking," he cautioned, "you and I can't become like Jesus, and this church can't become the body of Christ alive in the world." The life-giving ecclesial activities of worship, word, community, service, prayer, and mission are not things the church can do on its own power or by itself. It is possible to go through the motions, just as it is possible from a scientific standpoint to give intricate, anatomical explanations of what makes a body function. "But ultimately, life is a mystery," Phil reminded the assembly. Just as physical, embodied life is a gift from God, so too is the ability of the church to act as the body of Christ purely a gift of the Spirit. "And so, we must pray," he continued. "We must acknowledge that our life comes from God. We must cry out to God for his life-giving Spirit, for the Spirit of Christ to fill us, and to make our actions meaningful, to make them life-giving. All the rest is a mere gimmick, a mere new way of talking about things, if it's not filled with the life-giving Spirit of God." Phil's Trinitarian emphasis is significant and in keeping with the point made in

Chapter Two: the phenomena of church life do not constitute the communion of saints *ex opere operato;* rather, the church becomes what it is solely through the animation of the Spirit.

The church's ecclesial motto intrigued me, especially insofar as its rejection of disembodied gnostic soteriology offered the potential for constructive ecumenical dialogue. For example, Frank Senn proposes four theological criteria necessary for orthodox Christian worship. Orthodox Christian worship must be "explicitly Trinitarian," its "core content" must be Christological, and it must be "incarnational" and "eschatological" in scope.[5] West Shore's worship meets all four requirements. It is explicitly Trinitarian: one example is Phil's pastoral prayer, which is addressed to Jesus, who sits at the right hand of the Father and sends his Spirit upon the church. The core content of the service is Christological. This fact is highlighted throughout the service, but especially in the Scripture reading from Philippians ("At the name of Jesus, every knee should bow in heaven and on earth and under the earth, and every tongue confess that Jesus Christ is Lord, to the glory of God the Father"), and in the extended congregational song of reflection on Christ's name:

> Your name, all creation knows;/The One who gave it life with breath alone;/Your name./Your name, glory now displayed./All the earth belongs to You alone./Your name, Your name./And the mountains bow, and the seas will roar,/And the rocks cry out — all creation calls/to the Holy One, to the Son of God. We will lift our voice in praise./Worship Your name. Worship Your name.[6]

The incarnational and eschatological aspects of liturgy come through not only in this particular service, but also in the church's stated vision. The central passage of West Shore's ecclesiology — Romans 8:29 — speaks about the destiny of the believing community in language reminiscent of Genesis 1:26-27. If all human beings are created in the image of God, the writers of the New Testament emphasize that Jesus Christ *is* God's image, the firstborn of

---

5. Frank Senn, " 'Worship Alive': An Analysis and Critique of 'Alternative Worship,' " *Worship* 69, no. 3 (1995): 216.

6. Andy Bromley, "Your Name."

all creation. God's purpose for the new humanity and the new creation will be attained because in the one true human person, Jesus Christ, this goal has already been achieved.

Significantly, this reality is not reserved for the final consummation: "its power is operative in the here and now; the future is already present, albeit in a hidden manner, awaiting but also working towards its final revelation."[7] Ecclesiology is thus a Christological and an eschatological category, beautifully captured in West Shore's simple motto, "Becoming [eschatological] like Jesus [christological]." Indeed, the incarnational principle of "becoming like Jesus: head, heart, hands, knees, and feet" rejects gnosticism and affirms the post–Vatican II emphasis that "flesh and spirit, soul and body, are not competitors."[8]

At one point during the study, I pressed Phil about a potential weakness in the motto. I pointed out that head, heart, hands, knees, and feet are all components of each person's own body. One can work on strengthening them in the privacy of one's own home or in the company of fellow church members. But even if the latter is the ideal, the church becomes a gym — a gathering place for individuals randomly thrown together, who may or may not take encouragement from the fact that others in the room are sweating, and who have no real need to interact with one another to gain that which they came seeking. Recall, for example, the Johannine imagery of the previous chapter: "vine and branches" and "sheep in a flock" convey a different picture of collectivity than an image that sees each member as *dependent* on the other. Why does West Shore prioritize Romans 8 over 1 Corinthians 12 ("the eye cannot say to the hand, 'I don't need you!'"), when the latter conveys a stronger sense of mutual dependence?

Phil quickly nuanced my point by clarifying that West Shore does not make an either/or decision between Romans and 1 Corinthians. However, while the body metaphor in 1 Corinthians 12 talks about community, Phil stressed that for Paul, the phrase "in Christ," used so frequently throughout the book of Romans, best captures the essence of what it means to be a Christian. "The bigger biblical and theological concept," Phil emphasized,

7. Stanley J. Grenz, *The Social God and the Relational Self: A Trinitarian Theology of the Imago Dei* (Louisville and London: Westminster John Knox Press, 2001), p. 232.

8. Nathan Mitchell, *Meeting Mystery: Liturgy, Worship, Sacraments* (Maryknoll, N.Y.: Orbis Books, 2006), p. 161.

"is being made in the image of God, and Christ being the image of God. 'In Christ' comes first; the body metaphor is second."

As Phil demonstrated in a sermon about the Incarnation, West Shore makes continual, deliberate efforts to prevent personalism from devolving into individualism. In his teaching, Phil stresses that the act of incarnation, through which God became human, was an act of intimacy. Love and intimacy go hand in hand. To love is not just to want to be near, but to *insist* on being near — so near that "you feel like you can almost enter into the other person, to the point where their tears become your tears, their joys become your joys, their thoughts become your thoughts." This kind of intimacy, Phil suggests, is evident in the words of John, who refers to himself as "the disciple whom Jesus loved" and wrote about the incredible privilege it was to walk with Jesus in the flesh, look at him, and touch God in human form.

But God's intimacy with humanity extends even deeper than the Incarnation. Phil moves immediately to Pentecost, the day in which "God the Father and God the Son actually sent their very Spirit — their very inner life — into the disciples, and promised that from that day forward, everyone who believed would receive the very Spirit of the living God into their being, and would be able to live in union and communion with God the Father and God the Son through God the Holy Spirit." Incarnation and Pentecost together make intimacy with God and one another possible: God with us, so that God can enter into us, so that we can enter into the lives of others.

Liturgy, Grammar, and Language. I concluded the previous chapter by highlighting the plurality of Pentecost and the various grammars and syntaxes that undergird different human languages and liturgical languages alike. Christians do not learn the grammar of their faith primarily through Sunday school, catechism classes, or graduate seminars in theological method. Instead, through the weekly practice of the liturgy, individuals "become steeped in the Christian lexicon, formed by the Christian story, and capacitated to exercise the Christian grammar."[9] More simply: "Liturgy creates a Christian grammar in the people of God who live through the encounter with the paschal mystery."[10]

---

9. David W. Fagerberg, *Theologia Prima: What Is Liturgical Theology?* (Chicago: Liturgy Training Publications, 2003), p. 154; emphasis mine.

10. Fagerberg, *Theologia Prima*, p. 3.

Evangelicals can endorse many of these insights about the formative power of corporate ecclesial practices. Evangelical ecclesiology is "guided by Matthew 18:20, where Christ says, 'For where two or three are gathered in my name, I am there among them.' According to this text, Christ's presence is promised not to the believing individual directly, but rather to the entire congregation, and only through the latter to the individual."[11] Phil regularly reminds his congregation of precisely this fact:

> The Spirit comes to dwell in the body first — it's as two or three are gathered together that I am in your midst. We can't worship, in its full and proper sense, individually. We can't study and learn the Word individually. We obviously can't enter into community individually. We can't serve individually. The whole point of serving is that the charismata are distributed in such a way that we're all incomplete: it creates a forced interdependence. We can't pray individually: the Lord's Prayer is "we," not "I." We can't go on mission individually. We must manifest the deeds and the words of Jesus as a body together.

"It is from the church that one receives the content of faith, and it is in the church that one learns how faith is to be understood and lived."[12] Thus, there is wisdom in pressing the language of practice, habit, virtue, and ritual into service for Christian theology — especially since, as Peter Leithart points out, an "instinctive anti-ritualism" has left evangelicals "bereft of the theological tools required for understanding how rites sustain, mold, and nourish the church."[13]

West Shore's worship pattern — dubbed by choir director Doug as a "gentle liturgy" — is intentionally flexible and cannot be adequately described by the language of "rite." Doug explains, "Typically, there is a welcome/invocation/call to worship — I don't have one word for it, but it's an opening expression of our faith in worship that could be characterized by praise, thanksgiving, confession, or a combination of all three. It is typically

---

11. Miroslav Volf, *After Our Likeness: The Church as the Image of the Trinity* (Grand Rapids: Wm B. Eerdmans, 1998), p. 162.

12. Volf, *After Our Likeness*, p. 163.

13. Peter Leithart, "What's Wrong with Evangelical Theology?," *First Things* 65 (1996): 20.

marked by music. Then a pastoral prayer and the offering. Then [the] sermon. Then response, sending, benediction. Once a month we celebrate the
Lord's Supper." This structure is not inviolable. When the church was smaller,
every fifth Sunday of the month was given over to the congregation for public
testimony. There was no sermon those mornings — simply music, prayer,
and firsthand accounts of God's work in the life of the community. Last year,
as a short-term experiment, the church decided together to celebrate the
Lord's Supper weekly rather than monthly during the season of Lent.

While there is wisdom in practice, habit, and ritual, there is also something profoundly right about West Shore's refusal to prioritize inherited liturgical structure. No liturgy can render the reality of Christ in a wholly
accurate way because, as John Webster points out, "God's reality is not ex-
haustible in word or system." Webster stresses that the fundamental claim of
Christianity is that "its central subject and agent, Jesus, is *Lord:* that as this
particular human person, he is the one who shares in the mysterious and
utterly elusive absoluteness of God, and so defies any comprehension."[14] As
the one risen from the dead, sharing in the life of God, and present in the
outpoured Spirit, Jesus is "a fund of infinite potentiality."[15] Webster explains:

> Easter means that the history of the man Jesus embodies God's utter lib-
> erty: at his resurrection, Jesus assumes the limitless creativity of God,
> and thereby becomes infinitely potent in expanding our human history.
> The church exists by virtue of that liberty and potency. In them it finds a
> summons to a way of existing in which our capacity for wickedness and
> self-destruction is overcome and in which we are enabled to enter anew
> our human vocation. Do we have language for such freedom and power?
> Clearly not; all we have is language undergoing the process of conversion.
> "All language in Christ gains new meaning": so Luther. But new meaning
> emerges slowly, and with many mistakes — as routines are unlearned, as
> we begin to release language from our institutional grasp.[16]

14. John Webster, "Locality and Catholicity: Reflections on Theology and the Church,"
Scottish Journal of Theology 45 (1992): 10.

15. Webster, "Locality and Catholicity," p. 10.

16. John Webster, "The Church as Theological Community," *Anglican Theological Review*
75 (1993): 115.

In short, the church's life is more than simply the "socialization of subjects into a pre-structured semantic universe."[17] The reality of Jesus Christ cannot be "naturalized into the routines" of a cultural, linguistic, or liturgical system because it forever "runs ahead of our attempts to codify it."[18]

Cathy, a worship leader who has been with the congregation for almost thirty years, articulates this resistance to codification with an analogy. "West Shore has always been something like a petri dish. There's a culture for learning and growth. I have suggested things for worship, and some of them have failed . . . miserably!" she admits. "But the church continues to allow me to try things out in corporate worship, and all of us learn together. The congregation is always willing to take a chance with you, and to continue with you." She concludes by saying, "I think there's a seeking-ness about it. Seeking who the Lord is and what the Lord likes." Another interviewee, Nance, concurred:

> Worship here is not formulaic. There is no "equation." But there has been historically, and continues to be, a desire to seek after God with an authentic and sincere heart of worship and dependence. We manage to bring some things that are pretty different together in a way that still makes sense and continues to point us to God. This eclecticism makes worship exciting, and authentic, and maybe just enough of a conundrum to help us think more deeply about who God is.

West Shore's commitment to "seeking-ness" and eclecticism should not suggest that the church believes that Christianity is amorphous, open to indiscriminate interpretation. As Webster rightly stresses, the Christian gospel is "closed" in a crucial sense: its controlling center is "the 'unsubstitutable' career of Jesus of Nazareth, whose life, death, and resurrection are the enactment of God's final purposes for creation."[19] Jesus' "I am" declarations and the Johannine language of Christ as the world's "judgment" clearly demonstrate that "we are not at liberty to replace that controlling center [of the gospel] with something else."[20] The Christian imagination must constantly be

17. Webster, "Locality and Catholicity," p. 5.
18. Webster, "Locality and Catholicity," pp. 5, 12.
19. Webster, "Locality and Catholicity," p. 11.
20. Webster, "Locality and Catholicity," p. 11.

recalled to "*this* nameable reality, *this* sequence."[21] With this caution in place, Webster maintains that "the constraint on the range of possible renderings of this reality cannot be easily specified in advance."[22] Theology works for the good of the church in two ways: not only by reminding the church "of the specific lineaments of that center," but also by "[dissuading] the church from premature closure of the business of reading, receiving, and giving account of that which has brought it into being."[23]

Liturgical scholars excel at the former task — reminding the church of the lineaments of its center. Indeed, evangelicals' preference for speaking in a general way about "worship" rather than in a specific way about "liturgy" too often results in little critical engagement with the habits, forms, and patterns that congregations inevitably use. As John Witvliet rightly observes, it makes a difference if 90 percent of a congregation's sermons are inductive or deductive, if 90 percent of its sung music is linear or cyclical in form, if 90 percent of its prayers are offered for the needs of the congregation or the needs of the world.[24] Liturgical theologians' insistence that "the grammar of faith establishes itself in a life by its weekly exercise in liturgical rhythms" offers a healthy challenge to many evangelical theologies of worship.[25]

At the same time, congregations like West Shore excel at the task of dissuading the church from premature closure. Aidan Kavanagh and David Fagerberg distinguish the "natural" language of ordinary churchgoers from the "formalized" language of liturgical scholars. They charge the latter with the task of "parsing" the natural language the worshipping community speaks. In short, the liturgical theologian is a skilled inhabitant of a particular universe of discourse, a professional grammarian who is agile in displaying the community's use. However, Webster points out a problem inherent in this description: when the only stance of the theologian vis-à-vis the church is that of professional grammarian, "something essential to the community's health can be lost — namely, a lively, self-critical awareness

21. Webster, "Locality and Catholicity," p. 11.
22. Webster, "Locality and Catholicity," p. 11.
23. Webster, "Locality and Catholicity," p. 12.
24. John Witvliet, "From 'DNA' to 'Cellular Structure': Charting Recent Evangelical Scholarly Engagement with Corporate Worship Practices," in *The Serious Business of Worship*, ed. Melanie C. Ross and Simon Jones (London: T&T Clark, 2010), p. 200.
25. Fagerberg, *Theologia Prima*, p. 154.

of its own limits and what lies *outside* of them."[26] The danger of comparing liturgy to grammar is that the analogy tends to stress the "stable, 'regular' life of the church at the expense of its exploratory character."[27] West Shore stands as a powerful reminder that the full range of worshipful responses to the gospel cannot be specified in advance.

I am not suggesting that Free Churches are "catholic exceptions" whose protests are important to the overall health of the Christian faith, any more than I am suggesting that the Swedish language is a protest against Mandarin Chinese. Instead, I am advocating a shift in metaphor. Easter is a single, uncircumscribable language with a deeply Trinitarian, Christological, incarnational, and eschatological grammar. Every Sunday, churches like West Shore — no less than churches that follow a liturgical *ordo* — pray to unleash its power from their institutional grasp that they might better speak the truth afresh in their own distinctive local dialects.

---

26. Webster, "Locality and Catholicity," p. 5.
27. Webster, "Locality and Catholicity," p. 5.

On Defying a Dichotomy

*We would like American Protestants to articulate faith commitments
in more positive, less oppositional forms and formulas; to fight less
with each other while becoming more at home in our own religious
particularities; to be more attuned to the needs of the communities
in which we live, and less concerned about our competitive positions
in the American religious marketplace.*

Douglas Jacobsen and William Vance Trollinger Jr.,
Re-Forming the Center

A dichotomy is "a cutting in two; a division." While accurate, this benign
definition obscures an inherent tension: dichotomies take "the virtue of distinction, that is, the capacity to distinguish between things, and [extend] it
into opposition."[1] Like the well curve discussed in the Introduction, dichotomies deny the possibility of middle ground. They divide a spectrum into
one term and its opposite, with no possibility of a term that is neither one
nor the other, or that is both.[2] Simply put, dichotomies allow one privileged
term to determine the other. Instead of distinguishing between something
(A) and something else (B), a dichotomy formulates a distinction between

1. Raia Prokhovnik, *Rational Woman: A Feminist Critique of Dichotomy* (Manchester:
Manchester University Press, 2002), p. 23.
2. Prokhovnik, *Rational Woman*, p. 31.

something (A) and its opposite (not-A). Whatever is not-A becomes defined solely by the fact that it is not the same as A, rather than for itself or in its own terms.[3]

The complexity of the American religious scene seems to require dichotomous classifications: Catholic and Protestant, Northern and Southern, liberal and conservative, urban and rural, and, as the title of this book suggests, evangelical and liturgical. Dichotomies are, perhaps, inevitable. It is much easier to mobilize people by dividing the world in two and presenting one's own group as standing against an easily identified enemy. Mark Ellingsen points out that not so long ago, mainline Protestants defined themselves over against Catholics (and vice versa), and worshippers in confessionally oriented churches (e.g., Lutherans) defined themselves over against Protestants who were not confessional (e.g., Methodists, Baptists). He continues:

> In the ecumenical climate since the Second Vatican Council, this way of defining one's Christian identity over against other Christians has become bad (ecclesiastical) manners. And yet in an era like ours in which the weakening impact of our social and ecclesiastical institutions has made identity a precarious thing, ecumenically oriented Christians have tended to look to the Religious Right as a way of defining themselves. "We mainline Christians are not like those Fundies and Evangelicals," we say. Conservative Evangelicals are just as likely to define themselves over against those (mainline ecumenical) "liberals."[4]

Dichotomies are part and parcel of what Deborah Tannen, professor of linguistics at Georgetown University, has aptly named America's "argument culture":

> The argument culture urges us to approach the world — and the people in it — in an adversarial frame of mind. It rests on the assumption that

---

3. Hanneke Canters and Grace M. Jantzen, *Forever Fluid: A Reading of Luce Irigaray's "Elemental Passions"* (Manchester: Manchester University Press, 2006), p. 19.

4. Mark Ellingsen, "What's the Point of an Ecumenical-Evangelical Dialogue?" *MidStream* 37, no. 2 (1998): 214.

opposition is the best way to get anything done: the best way to discuss an idea is to set up a debate; the best way to cover news is to find spokespeople who express the most extreme, polarized views and present them as "both sides"; the best way to settle disputes is litigation that pits one party against the other; the best way to begin an essay is to attack someone; and the best way to show you're really thinking is to criticize.[5]

Closely related to this polarization is our cultural obsession with rankings. Magazines supply lists of the "10, 50, or 100 best of everything," and ratings "pit restaurants, products, schools, and people against each other on a single scale, obscuring the myriad differences among them." Even after important political debates, "analysts comment not on what the candidates said but on the question 'Who won?'"[6] Too often, this seems true of worship discussions as well: one headline announces that mainlines are losing congregants to megachurches; another proclaims that megachurches are losing disenchanted youth who seek out ancient practices.

Polarization is alluring: it easily and naturally arouses interest. But stirring up animosities can "open old wounds or create new ones that are hard to heal."[7] Tannen rightly points out that "when our eagerness to find weaknesses blinds us to strengths; when the atmosphere of animosity precludes respect and poisons our relations with one another; then the argument culture is doing more damage than good."[8] We need a new kind of evangelical/liturgical dialogue, one that celebrates common ground, allows honest, genuine disagreement, and seeks out local middle ground.

Celebrating Common Ground

Of course, it is true that in one sense *all* churches are both liturgical and evangelical. Constance Cherry points out that liturgy "is not a 'bad' or 'good' word." "It is simply a word — a biblical word that reminds us that whatever

5. Deborah Tannen, *The Argument Culture: Stopping America's War of Words* (New York: Ballantine Books, 1998), p. 3.

6. Tannen, *The Argument Culture*, p. 22.

7. Tannen, *The Argument Culture*, p. 7.

8. Tannen, *The Argument Culture*, p. 25.

worship acts we offer to God constitute our liturgy."[9] Lester Ruth explains that in its biblical context, *leitourgia* can refer "both to Christ's work on humanity's behalf" (Heb. 8:1-2) and "the church's participation as the body of Christ in the ongoing ministry of Christ for all people." Therefore, it is poor theology to limit "liturgical" to one formalized ceremonial style of worship: *all* worship must be "liturgical" (in the Hebrews 8 sense of the word) to be truly Christian. Ruth concludes, "The theological question is not whether any certain kind of Christian worship is liturgical or not, but *how* it is liturgical."[10]

The corollary claim — that all churches are evangelical — proceeds along the same methodological lines. When Robert Webber traces the origins of evangelicalism, he begins with the Greek word *euangelion,* a word that means "good news, good tidings, or gospel." Webber is aware that "the exclusive use of the term *evangelical* by some American Protestants (as if they were the only Christians focused on the *evangel*) can appear presumptuous if not arrogant to Christians from other traditions." Therefore, Webber defines an evangelical as simply "anyone who believes in the message that the death and resurrection of Jesus Christ is the good news of the forgiveness of sin, the inauguration of a new humanity."[11] An evangelical can belong to any church: "Catholic, Eastern Orthodox, one of the major Protestant denominations, or any of the many churches which stand in the free church tradition."[12] According to Webber, the only groups within Christian history that are to be excluded from the definition of "evangelical" are "those who so thoroughly reinterpret it through their conceptual grid (i.e., Gnostics, anti-supernatural liberals) that it ceases to retain integrity with apostolic intent."[13] Webber's definition of *evangelical* is broad enough to include almost any Christian.

I celebrate the common ground that can be gained by returning to the

9. Constance Cherry, *The Worship Architect: A Blueprint for Designing Culturally Relevant and Biblically Faithful Services* (Grand Rapids: Baker, 2010), p. 39.

10. Lester Ruth, "A Rose by Any Other Name," in *The Conviction of Things Not Seen: Worship and Ministry in the Twenty-First Century,* ed. Todd Johnson (Grand Rapids: Brazos Press, 2002), p. 42.

11. Robert E. Webber, *Common Roots: A Call to Evangelical Maturity* (Grand Rapids: Zondervan, 1978), p. 33.

12. Webber, *Common Roots,* p. 25.

13. Robert E. Webber, "An Evangelical and Catholic Methodology," in *The Use of the Bible in Theology: Evangelical Options,* ed. Robert K. Johnston (Atlanta: John Knox Press, 1985), p. 152.

scriptural roots of *leitourgia* and *euangelion*. But at the same time, it must be recognized that both terms have accrued significant layers of historical meaning in subsequent centuries. For better or for worse, when nonspecialists hear the word *liturgy*, they think of a textual tradition that includes the Sunday liturgy of word and sacrament, the worship practices of particular denominations (e.g., the liturgy of the Church of England, the liturgy of the Roman Catholic Church, etc.), or very specific ancient rites (e.g., "The Liturgy of St. Basil," "The Liturgy of St. John Chrysostom"). Some evangelical congregations intentionally distance themselves from the elements and patterns that characterize this tradition of worship.

The word *evangelical* is even more problematic. Timothy Larsen points out that the "politeness" of defining the evangelical camp in a way that includes Roman Catholic and Eastern orthodox believers "has the liability of being apt to confuse the uninitiated."[14] Furthermore, when Boston sociologist Alan Wolfe proclaimed, "We're all evangelicals now," it was not an affirmation that all Christians are witnesses to the good news of the gospel.[15] Instead, he was suggesting that many characteristics of twentieth-century evangelicalism — its therapeutic tendencies, market-savvy approaches to church growth, and even a certain theological fuzziness — had permeated other faith traditions in America, including Roman Catholicism and Judaism. Because the biblical words *leitourgia* and *euangelion* have such a complex history in common parlance and the popular imagination, it may not be possible to engage them with the first naïveté that ecumenical scholarship seems to assume.

Can common ground still be recovered when scholars press beyond this "first naïveté" of etymological origins to a "second naïveté" that acknowledges the definitional shifts in both words over the course of time? The response of this book is a resounding "Yes!" Evangelical and liturgical scholars alike share a commitment to ecumenism, a nuanced understanding of Scripture that eschews fundamentalism, and a desire to think together about issues of ecclesiology and sacraments. "Low church" evangelical congregations

14. Timothy Larsen, "Defining and Locating Evangelicalism," in *The Cambridge Companion to Evangelical Theology*, ed. Timothy Larsen and Daniel J. Treier (Cambridge: Cambridge University Press, 2007), p. 4.

15. Alan Wolfe, *The Transformation of American Religion: How We Actually Live Our Faith* (New York: Free Press, 2004), p. 36.

share with their "high church" liturgical counterparts a history of careful thought about how to ground worship in Scripture; a theological commitment to worship that is Trinitarian, incarnational, and eschatological; and an insistence on an indissoluble interrelation between worship and ethics. These commonalities have too long been obscured by critiques of Finney's threefold *ordo,* and their recovery is cause for celebration.

Acknowledging Genuine Disagreement

To celebrate commonality is not to deny or flatten differences. Churches do disagree about important topics, including the theology of ordinances (evangelical) or sacraments (liturgical) and the frequency of their celebration. However, genuine disagreement is not cause for despair. As Nancy Bedford suggests, it may, in fact, be salutary to the health of the church:

> It seems to me that what is particularly promising for theology is not primarily the prospect of the amiable dialogue of birds of a feather, though at times such may be needed, but also the challenge of tense, messy conversations along the way with those who are or may become our friends. As in the case of the disciples on the road to Emmaus, who were "talking and arguing among themselves" (Luke 24:15), in the midst of heated conversation we may unexpectedly find Jesus walking along with us — and our theology will be the better for it.[16]

Of course, as I noted in Chapter Four, every church must, at minimum, be open to all other churches that make a confession of faith — even those churches with whom they may vehemently disagree. Just as importantly, this openness ought not to be grudging. Don Saliers and Henry H. Knight III express this point beautifully in their co-authored book, *The Conversation Matters:* "How we treat one another in the midst of controversy is not a sign of how strongly we are committed to our position, but how deeply we are

---

16. Nancy Bedford, "Speak, 'Friend,' and Enter: Friendship and Theological Method," in *God's Life in Trinity,* ed. Miroslav Volf and Michael Welker (Minneapolis: Fortress Press, 2006), p. 43.

committed to Jesus Christ. For it is 'By this everyone will know that you are my disciples, if you have love for one another.'"[17]

In this irenic spirit, allow me to suggest two areas of disagreement that merit future treatment. The first concerns the *telos* of ecumenism. In his 1989 McCarthy Lecture, George Lindbeck distinguished between two kinds of ecumenists. The first group, "unitive ecumenists," ground their renewal efforts in sacraments and *ressourcement* — a return to the church's biblical and patristic roots. The unitive style of ecumenism presided at the formation of the World Council of Churches and recognizes the Lima document — *Baptism, Eucharist, and Ministry* (1982) — as a high point in ecumenical relations.[18] The document reminds the churches that sharing in "one bread and the common cup in a given place" not only demonstrates but also *"effects* the oneness of the sharers with Christ and with their fellow sharers in all times and places. It is in the Eucharist that the community of God's people is fully manifested."[19] Similarly, a 1997 Faith and Order paper stresses that we have all been brought into Christ through our common baptism: "Because Christ has claimed us, we have no right to reject one another."[20]

In direct contrast, Lindbeck's second group, "interdenominational ecumenists," are at best "indifferent" to the ecumenical movement or, at worst, "have a distinct antipathy to spending time and effort on working for the union of churches." Lindbeck explains the reason for their aversion: it "is not because they are parochially Methodist, Anglican, Presbyterian, Lutheran, or Baptist," but rather because "the whole question of ecclesial identity and unification is for them a distraction from the one thing necessary, the saving of individual souls."[21] Lindbeck's definition of the second group requires more nuance: as I suggested in Chapter One, evangelicals are neither averse

17. Henry H. Knight III and Don E. Saliers, *The Conversation Matters: Why United Methodists Should Talk with One Another* (Nashville: Abingdon Press, 1999), p. 73.

18. George A. Lindbeck, "Two Kinds of Ecumenism: Unitive and Interdenominational," *Gregorianum* 70, no. 4 (1989): 654.

19. World Council of Churches, *Baptism, Eucharist, and Ministry*, Faith and Order Paper 111 (Geneva: World Council of Churches, 1982), p. 19.

20. *Becoming a Christian: The Ecumenical Implications of Our Common Baptism*, Faith and Order Paper 184, ed. Thomas F. Best and Dagmar Heller (Geneva: World Council of Churches, 1999), p. 3.

21. Lindbeck, "Two Kinds of Ecumenism," p. 653.

to nor indifferent to an ecumenism grounded in the experience of new birth. Given that caveat, the questions that Lindbeck raises about the relationship between evangelism, soteriology, and sacramental practice are salient and deserve sustained attention.

A second topic for future evangelical/liturgical dialogue concerns the role of critical biblical scholarship in Christian worship. D. G. Hart observes a paradox in American religion: "The most vocal defenders of traditional family values [evangelicals] are also the most active proponents of liturgical innovations."[22] Taking Hart's observation a step further, the evangelical congregations who champion liturgical innovation are also the most likely to read Scripture traditionally. Consider the reflections of a guest preacher at Eastbrook:

> When you look at the Bible, there is internal evidence that it's a strong, reliable historical document. It's written primarily by eyewitnesses. Moses was there when the Red Sea split, and he wrote about it. Joshua was there when the walls of Jericho fell down, and he wrote about it. The disciples of Jesus were standing in the Upper Room when Jesus, who had died, was resurrected and suddenly was standing in that room with them, and they wrote about it. It's a list of eyewitness accounts about what God did.

In an interview at West Shore, Phil, the senior pastor, prefaced his remarks about Scripture with a qualifying statement:

> Now, do I realize the Bible is a historical product, that there are levels of tradition, that there's incorporating of ancient, outmoded points of view? For example, when I read Genesis 1, am I going to get caught up in the debate for six 24-hour days of creation? Absolutely not. I think the author of Genesis was operating with an Ancient Near Eastern cosmology, and my view of inspiration doesn't protect me from that.

Yet Phil made it clear that he accepts a conservative interpretation of passages that modern biblical scholarship might question:

22. D. G. Hart, *The Lost Soul of American Protestantism* (Lanham, Md.: Rowman & Littlefield, 2004), p. 144.

I read the Gospel narratives in a fairly straightforward, literal way. I see them as theological documents where things are selected and organized to make a point, but I don't think they're legends. I think Jesus *actually* walked on water. I think Peter did too. The Bible is true, and I have not encountered anything in modern scholarship that has caused me to be shaken from that.

It is interesting to compare the words of these pastors with recent work by liturgical scholars Gordon Lathrop and Gail Ramshaw. In his book *Four Gospels on Sunday*, Lathrop writes that the Gospels "are not primarily historical reports about Jesus, not documents working out differing views of what Jesus may have been like in his life, not invitations to imagine what actually happened then." Indeed, "they would be diminished if they were construed as historical reports rather than as fascinating and profound poetic constructions around issues of immense religious import." Although the Gospels "do give accounts of a real person who acted and who was cruelly killed in a real place and time," Lathrop suggests that they are best understood as "announcements of Jesus-then becoming Jesus-now, especially Jesus-now in assembly." The Gospels "evidence the faith that this person still remains encounterable and that those actions and that death matter profoundly now, in the assembly where the books are being read."[23]

Gail Ramshaw similarly rejects literalistic interpretations of Scripture: "I have endured far too many sermons that elaborate what Jesus was feeling at some event that never took place." Accordingly, she challenges homileticians to "preach in a way that remains faithful to the critical biblical studies to which you subscribe."[24] Ramshaw poses the same challenge to herself: "What are my obligations as a writer of liturgical prayer? If a liturgical prayer thanks God for saving Noah from the flood, will worshippers assume that the flood was a historical fact?" Relatedly: "To keep from literalism, is it helpful for the prayer to thank God for 'the stories of Abraham and Sarah'"? Moving to the New Testament, Ramshaw notes,

23. Gordon Lathrop, *The Four Gospels on Sunday: The New Testament and the Reform of Christian Worship* (Minneapolis: Fortress Press, 2011), p. 154.

24. Gail Ramshaw, "A Conversation with Julian of Norwich about Liturgical Language," *Worship* 85, no. 1 (2011): 12.

In the past, most Christian theologians claimed that Jesus really spoke [the words of institution] at an historical event on the Thursday before he was executed and that this meal instituted a Christian ritual to be repeated in perpetuity. Now, many mainstream New Testament scholars reject such historical literalism, and I ask liturgists not to invoke a literalism to which they do not subscribe.[25]

Ramshaw, Lathrop, and the congregations of Eastbrook and West Shore share the same confession of faith. All understand the robust proclamation of the gospel as vital to the mission of the church. Yet even a cursory summation of their positions makes clear that genuine disagreement between them is undeniable. Space prohibits further treatment of this important topic, but differences between "liberal" and "conservative" interpretations of Scripture in worship are likely to invite lively and fruitful liturgical/evangelical dialogue for many years to come.

Seeking Local Middle Ground

What would a nondichotomous evangelical/liturgical relationship look like in practice? There is no shortage of practical resources or theoretical blueprints available to churches seeking to forge this *via media*. In 2002, Lester Ruth offered a tongue-in-cheek survey of the field:

How would you classify the worship of your church or parish? Is it "contemporary" or "traditional"? Are those forms too limited? In that case, would the terms "linear" or "organic," as found in some recent youth ministry training materials, be more helpful? Still at a loss for the right classification? Maybe the terms from a recent online worship forum would be more accurate: "multisensory worship," "indigenous worship," "innovative worship," "transformational worship," "blended worship," "praise services," "spirited traditional," "creative," or "classic worship"?[26]

25. Ramshaw, "A Conversation with Julian of Norwich about Liturgical Language," p. 13.
26. Ruth, "A Rose by Any Other Name," p. 33.

The thirteen options cited above are only the tip of the iceberg. Ruth's extended list continues to include ethnically designated ("African American," "Hispanic," "Euro-American") and generationally based ("boomer," "buster," "Gen-X," "millennials") options. Were the list updated today, it might also include emerging church and liquid worship models,[27] as well as worship models based on specific passages of Scripture (e.g., "Solomon's Worship," based on the temple dedication of 2 Chronicles 5–7, or "Spiritual Worship," based on Romans 11–15, to cite but two of many possible examples).[28]

Models and blueprints are invaluable: they orient participants to a shared ultimate reality. However, Nicholas Healy observes that blueprints are problematic insofar as they give the impression that "it is necessary to get our thinking about the church right first, after which we can go on to put our theory into practice."[29] Put differently, blueprints undervalue the struggle of living in a less-than-perfect church, which leads to discouragement:

> In our modern world we have the tendency to begin with a theory and then try to translate it into practice. When something is not working, we theorize about why and then come up with another theoretical model and try to put *it* into action. We . . . think, read, talk, discuss, idealize, blog, and suggest endlessly what the church *should* be, and we give our new dreams of church creative names and then categorize them; but we just as often fail to make them concrete reality.[30]

Healy points out that Christianity is too richly multifaceted to be fully contained within any single system. To treat Christian faith and worship as if

27. See Bryan D. Spinks, *The Worship Mall: Contemporary Responses to Contemporary Culture* (London: SPCK, 2010).

28. See Bryan Chapell, *Christ-Centered Worship: Letting the Gospel Shape Our Practice* (Grand Rapids: Baker, 2009).

29. Nicholas M. Healy, *Church, World, and Christian Life: Practical-Prophetic Ecclesiology* (Cambridge: Cambridge University Press, 2000), p. 36.

30. Jason Clark, "Consumer Liturgies and Their Corrosive Effects on Christian Identity," in *Church in Present Tense: A Candid Look at What's Emerging*, ed. Scot McKnight, Kevin Corcoran, Peter Rollins, and Jason Clark (Grand Rapids: Brazos Press, 2011), p. 47.

they had "a definable essence, a single principle in terms of which one could systematically map the whole, is inevitably to distort it."[31]

Although there is no universal blueprint for overcoming the evangelical/liturgical dichotomy, this book celebrates the fact that middle ground is regularly being forged at local levels. To find it, liturgical scholars must occasionally trade in the drafting board of an architect for the walking shoes of a pedestrian. An analogy from Jesuit scholar Michel de Certeau helps illustrate this point. Imagine an architectural model of a city enclosed under glass, perhaps with tiny human figures added to the scene for scale. From this bird's-eye view, there is a particular logic to the city: it is "laid out, legible, resolved. One can see how things relate to each other, put certain markers in place, take in distances across the city in a single sweep."[32] Now imagine the same city from the street-level perspective of a pedestrian. Pedestrians may take shortcuts or wander aimlessly rather than following the utilitarian layout of street grids. Their outlook continually changes as they walk, "deftly avoiding traffic, sidestepping and negotiating their way around obstacles, ignoring the honking, but noticing the displays on the sidewalk, passing by, reaching towards and generally 'muddling through' on their way to work."[33] In short, pedestrians "reappropriate" the city of architects and planners according to their own interests and rules.

As with pedestrians, so too with congregations. While there is nothing wrong with drafting or consulting blueprints, "pedestrian" theologies of worship are negotiated from within a local context that includes "the church's history, both local and worldwide; the background beliefs and the economic and social status of its members; recent developments among its leaderships; [and] styles of argumentation in theology."[34] Pedestrian theologies of worship do not transfer wholesale from one context to another. As John Witvliet observes, "In one congregation, a new Gen X service might arise out of genuine spiritual renewal and a desire for deeper worship. In another, it might signal a desire for a less demanding form of worship." Similarly,

---

31. Healy, *Church, World, and Christian Life,* p. 35.

32. Cited in Fran Tonkiss, *Space, the City, and Social Theory: Social Relations and Urban Forms* (Cambridge: Polity Press, 2005), p. 127.

33. Robert C. H. Chia and Robin Holt, *Strategy without Design: The Silent Efficacy of Indirect Action* (Cambridge: Cambridge University Press, 2009), p. 148.

34. Healy, *Church, World, and Christian Life,* p. 39.

One congregation's addition of a praise team and PowerPoint presentational software might lead to greater lay participation in worship and services that are pastorally, theologically, and spiritually richer. Another's identical innovation might lead to less engagement, less congregational participation, and reduced theological and spiritual content.[35]

Though they may be nontransferable, local theologies need not be myopic. Local communities are impelled to move outward: they must "make some contribution to the way in which the whole of the Christian church understands itself, either by affirming what is already known in the tradition or by extending it to new circumstances."[36] Theologian Daniel Migliore rightly concludes that "responsible local theology must be ecumenical in intent even as truly ecumenical theology must be open to the insights and calls to action that come from local theologies."[37]

This is a challenging agenda, to say the least. But it is one that countless congregations across the country enthusiastically embrace each week. In Pennsylvania, a West Shore interviewee summed up matters this way: "I hope your book won't just be about a couple of evangelical churches. I hope it will be something that speaks to the church universal." This, in a nutshell, is my hope as well.

---

35. John Witvliet, "Beyond Style: Asking Deeper Questions about Worship," *Congregations* 27, no. 4 (July/August 2001): 19-21, 35.

36. Robert J. Schreiter, *Constructing Local Theologies* (Maryknoll, N.Y.: Orbis Books, 1986), p. 120.

37. Daniel L. Migliore, *Faith Seeking Understanding: An Introduction to Christian Theology* (Grand Rapids: Wm. B. Eerdmans, 1991), p. 221.

Bibliography

Allert, Craig D. *A High View of Scripture? The Authority of the Bible and the Forma-tion of the New Testament Canon.* Grand Rapids: Baker Academic, 2007.

Ammerman, Nancy T. *Pillars of Faith: American Congregations and Their Partners.* Berkeley and Los Angeles: University of California Press, 2005.

Anderson, Paul N. *The Christology of the Fourth Gospel: Its Unity and Disunity in the Light of John 6.* Tübingen: J. C. B. Mohr, 1996.

Aune, Michael B. "Liturgy and Theology: Rethinking the Relationship, Part I." *Worship* 81, no. 1 (2007): 46-68.

————. "Protestant Worship: Traditions in Transition." *Theological Studies* 51 (1990): 791-92.

Bedford, Nancy Elizabeth. "Speak 'Friend,' and Enter: Friendship and Theological Method." In *God's Life in Trinity,* edited by Miroslav Volf and Michael Welker, pp. 33-43. Minneapolis: Fortress Press, 2006.

Beneke, Chris. *Beyond Toleration: The Religious Origins of American Pluralism.* New York: Oxford University Press, 2006.

Best, Harold M. "A Traditional Worship Response" to Robert Webber's "Blended Worship" chapter. In *Exploring the Worship Spectrum: Six Views,* edited by Paul A. Basden. Grand Rapids: Zondervan, 2004.

Best, Thomas F., and Dagmar Heller, eds. *Becoming a Christian: The Ecumenical Im-plications of Our Common Baptism.* Faith and Order Paper 184. Geneva: World Council of Churches, 1999.

Bloesch, Donald G. *The Church: Sacraments, Worship, Ministry, Mission.* Downers Grove, Ill.: InterVarsity Press, 2002.

Bradshaw, Paul F. "Difficulties in Doing Liturgical Theology." *Pacifica* 11 (1998): 181-94.

————. "The Homogenization of Christian Liturgy — Ancient and Modern." *Studia Liturgica* 26 (1996): 1-15.

Brand, Eugene. "Berakah Response: Ecumenism and the Liturgy." *Worship* 58 (1984): 305-15.

Brinkman, M. E. *Progress in Unity? Fifty Years of Theology within the World Council of Churches: 1945-1995.* Leuven: Peeters Press, 1995.

Brown, Raymond E. *The Churches the Apostles Left Behind.* New York: Paulist Press, 1984.

————. *The Community of the Beloved Disciple.* New York: Paulist Press, 1979.

Bruner, F. D. *A Theology of the Holy Spirit.* Grand Rapids: Wm. B. Eerdmans, 1970.

Burgess, John P. *Why Scripture Matters.* Louisville: Westminster John Knox Press, 1998.

Canters, Hanneke, and Grace Jantzen. *Forever Fluid: A Reading of Luce Irigaray's "Elemental Passions."* Manchester: Manchester University Press, 2005.

Carpenter, Joel. "The Scope of American Evangelicalism: Some Comments on the Marsden-Dayton Exchange." *Christian Scholar's Review* 23, no. 1 (1993): 53-61.

Castro, Emilio. "Ecumenism and Evangelicalism: Where Are We?" In *Faith and Faithfulness: Essays on Contemporary Ecumenical Themes — A Tribute to Phillip A. Potter,* edited by Pauline Webb. Geneva: World Council of Churches, 1984.

Chan, Simon. *Liturgical Theology: The Church as Worshiping Community.* Downers Grove, Ill.: IVP Academic, 2006.

Chauvet, Louis-Marie. *The Sacraments: The Word of God at the Mercy of the Body.* Collegeville, Minn.: Liturgical Press, 2001.

————. *Symbol and Sacrament: A Sacramental Reinterpretation of Christian Existence.* Collegeville, Minn.: Liturgical Press, 1995.

Cherry, Constance. *The Worship Architect: A Blueprint for Designing Culturally Relevant and Biblically Faithful Services.* Grand Rapids: Baker, 2010.

Chia, Robert C. H., and Robin Holt. *Strategy without Design: The Silent Efficacy of Indirect Action.* Cambridge: Cambridge University Press, 2009.

Clark, Matthew S. "Pentecostalism's Anabaptist Roots: Hermeneutical Implications." In *The Spirit and Spirituality: Essays in Honour of Russell P. Spittler,* edited by Wonsuk Ma and Robert P. Menzies. London: T&T Clark International, 2004.

Cosgrove, Charles H. "The Place Where Jesus Is: Allusions to Baptism and the Eucharist in the Fourth Gospel." *New Testament Studies* 35, no. 4 (1989): 522-39.

Daniels III, David D., and Ted A. Smith. "History, Practice, and Theological Education." In *For Life Abundant: Practical Theology, Theological Education, and Christian Ministry,* edited by Dorothy C. Bass and Craig Dykstra, pp. 214-40. Grand Rapids: Wm. B. Eerdmans, 2008.

Dayton, Donald W. *Discovering an Evangelical Heritage.* New York: Harper & Row, 1976.

————. "Rejoinder to the Historiographical Discussion." *Christian Scholar's Review* 23, no. 1 (1993): 62-71.

————. "The Search for the Historical Evangelicalism: George Marsden's History of Fuller Seminary as a Case Study." *Christian Scholar's Review* 23, no. 1 (1993): 12-33.

————. "Yet Another Layer of the Onion, Or Opening the Ecumenical Door to Let the Riffraff in." *The Ecumenical Review* 40, no. 1 (1988): 87-110.

DeSilva, David A. *An Introduction to the New Testament.* Downers Grove, Ill.: Inter-Varsity Press, 2004.

Dorrien, Gary. *The Word as True Myth: Interpreting Modern Theology.* Louisville: Westminster John Knox Press, 1997.

Dulles, Avery. "Church, Ministry, and Sacraments in Catholic-Evangelical Dialogue." In *Catholics and Evangelicals: Do They Share a Common Future?*, edited by Thomas Rausch. New York: Paulist Press, 2000.

Dunn, James D. G. "John and the Synoptics as a Theological Question." In *Exploring the Gospel of John: In Honor of D. Moody Smith*, edited by R. Alan Culpepper and C. Clifton Black. Louisville: Westminster John Knox Press, 1996.

Dyrness, William A. "Spaces for an Evangelical Ecclesiology." In *The Community of the Word: Toward an Evangelical Ecclesiology*, edited by Mark Husbands and Daniel J. Treier. Downers Grove, Ill.: InterVarsity Press, 2005.

Ellingsen, Mark. "What's the Point of an Ecumenical-Evangelical Dialogue?" *Mid-Stream* 37, no. 2 (1998): 213-29.

Ellis, Christopher. *Gathering: A Theology and Spirituality of Worship in Free Church Tradition.* London: SCM Press, 2004.

Fagerberg, David W. *Theologia Prima: What Is Liturgical Theology?* Chicago: Hillenbrand Books, 2004.

————. *What Is Liturgical Theology? A Study in Methodology.* Yonkers, N.Y.: Pueblo Publishing Co., 1992.

Fenwick, John, and Bryan Spinks. *Worship in Transition: The Liturgical Movement in the Twentieth Century.* New York: Continuum, 1995.

Ferreira, John. *Johannine Ecclesiology.* Sheffield: Sheffield Academic Press, 1998.

Finke, Roger, and Rodney Stark. *The Churching of America, 1776-1990.* New Brunswick: Rutgers University Press, 1992.

Finney, Charles Grandison. *Lectures on Revivals of Religion.* Cambridge: Belknap Press of Harvard University Press, 1960.

Gassmann, Günter. "Scripture, Tradition, and the Church: The Ecumenical Nexus in Faith and Order Work." Unpublished manuscript, Melbourne, 1992.

George, Timothy. "The Sacramentality of the Church: An Evangelical Baptist Perspective." *Pro Ecclesia* 12, no. 3 (2003): 309-23.

Gerstner, John H. "The Theological Boundaries of Evangelical Faith." In *The Evan-*

gelicals: What They Believe, Who They Are, Where They Are Changing, edited
by David F. Wells and John D. Woodbridge. Nashville: Abingdon Press, 1975.

Gooder, Paula. "'According to the Scriptures . . ': The Use of the Bible in *Baptism,
Eucharist, and Ministry.*" In *Paths to Unity: Explorations in Ecumenical Method,*
edited by Paul Avis. London: Church House Publishing, 2004.

Grenz, Stanley J. *The Social God and the Relational Self: A Trinitarian Theology of the
Imago Dei.* Louisville and London: Westminster John Knox Press, 2001.

Grisbrooke, W. Jardine. "An Orthodox Approach to Liturgical Theology: The Work of
Alexander Schmemann." *Studia Liturgica* 23, no. 2 (1993): 140-57.

Gundry, Robert H. *Jesus the Word according to John the Sectarian: A Paleofundamentalist Manifesto for Contemporary Evangelicalism, Especially Its Elites, in North
America.* Grand Rapids: Wm. B. Eerdmans, 2002.

Hart, D. G. *The Lost Soul of American Protestantism.* Lanham, Md.: Rowman & Littlefield, 2004.

———. *Recovering Mother Kirk: The Case for Liturgy in the Reformed Tradition.*
Grand Rapids: Baker, 2003.

———. "Why Evangelicals Think They Hate Liturgy." *Modern Reformation* 5 (1996):
17-20.

Hauerwas, Stanley M. "Worship, Evangelism, Ethics: On Eliminating the 'And.'" In
Liturgy and the Moral Self: Humanity at Full Stretch before God, edited by E. Byron Anderson and Bruce T. Morrill. Collegeville, Minn.: Liturgical Press, 1998.

Healy, Nicholas M. *Church, World, and Christian Life: Practical-Prophetic Ecclesiology.* Cambridge: Cambridge University Press, 2000.

Hervieu-Léger, Danièle. "Individualism, the Validation of Faith, and the Social Nature of Religion in Modernity." In *The Blackwell Companion to the Sociology of
Religion,* edited by Richard K. Fenn. Oxford: Blackwell, 2001.

Hindmarsh, Bruce. "Is Evangelical Ecclesiology an Oxymoron? A Historical Perspective." In *Evangelical Ecclesiology: Reality or Illusion?,* edited by John G. Stackhouse Jr. Grand Rapids: Baker, 2003.

Hocken, Peter. "Ecumenical Dialogue: The Importance of Dialogue with Evangelicals
and Pentecostals." *One in Christ* 30 (1994): 101-23.

Horton, Michael Scott. "The Battles over the Label 'Evangelical.'" *Modern Reformation*
10, no. 2 (2001): 15-21.

———. "Reflection: Is Evangelicalism Reformed or Wesleyan? Reopening the
Marsden-Dayton Debate." *Christian Scholar's Review* 31 (2001): 131-55.

Hughes, Graham. *Worship as Meaning: A Liturgical Theology for Late Modernity.*
Cambridge: Cambridge University Press, 2003.

Hutcheson, Richard G., Jr., and Peggy Shriver. *The Divided Church: Moving Liberals
and Conservatives from Diatribe to Dialogue.* Downers Grove, Ill.: InterVarsity
Press, 1999.

Irwin, Kevin W. *Context and Text: Method in Liturgical Theology.* Collegeville, Minn.: Liturgical Press, 1993.

———. *Models of the Eucharist.* Mahwah, N.J.: Paulist Press, 2005.

Jacobsen, Douglas, and William Vance Trollinger Jr., editors. *Re-Forming the Center: American Protestantism, 1900 to the Present.* Grand Rapids: Wm. B. Eerdmans, 1998.

Johnson, Maxwell. "Can We Avoid Relativism in Worship? Liturgical Norms in the Light of Contemporary Liturgical Scholarship." *Worship* 74 (2000): 135-55.

———. "Is Anything Normative in Contemporary Lutheran Worship?" In *The Serious Business of Worship: Essays in Honour of Bryan D. Spinks,* edited by Melanie C. Ross and Simon Jones. London: T&T Clark International, 2010.

———. "Liturgy and Theology." In *Liturgy in Dialogue: Essays in Memory of Ronald Jasper,* edited by Paul Bradshaw and Bryan Spinks. Collegeville, Minn.: Liturgical Press, 1993.

Jorns, Klaus-Peter. "Liturgy: Cradle of Scripture?" *Studia Liturgica* 22 (1992): 17-34.

Kärkkäinen, Veli-Matti. *An Introduction to Ecclesiology: Ecumenical, Historical, and Global Perspectives.* Downers Grove, Ill.: InterVarsity Press, 2002.

Kaufman, Gordon. "On the Meaning of 'Act of God.'" *Harvard Theological Review* 61 (1968): 175-201.

Kavanagh, Aidan. "Liturgy and Ecclesial Consciousness: A Dialectic of Change." *Studia Liturgica* 15 (1982/1983): 2-17.

———. *On Liturgical Theology.* Yonkers, N.Y.: Pueblo Publishing Co., 1992.

———. "Scripture and Worship in Synagogue and Church." *Michigan Quarterly Review* 22 (1983): 480-94.

———. *The Shape of Baptism: The Rite of Christian Initiation.* Yonkers, N.Y.: Pueblo Publishing Co., 1978.

Kelsey, David. *The Uses of Scripture in Recent Theology.* Philadelphia: Fortress Press, 1975.

Kidd, Thomas S. *The Great Awakening: The Roots of Evangelical Christianity in Colonial America.* New Haven: Yale University Press, 2007.

Kimball, Dan. "Responses to Timothy C. J. Quill, 'Liturgical Position.'" In *Perspectives on Christian Worship: Five Views,* edited by J. Matthew Pinson. Nashville: Broadman & Holman Publishers, 2009.

Knight, Henry H., and Don E. Saliers. *The Conversation Matters: Why United Methodists Should Talk with One Another.* Nashville: Abingdon Press, 1999.

Koester, Craig R. *Symbolism in the Fourth Gospel: Meaning, Mystery, Community.* Minneapolis: Fortress Press, 2003.

Kysar, Robert. *John, the Maverick Gospel.* Louisville: Westminster John Knox Press, 1993.

————. *Voyages with John: Charting the Fourth Gospel.* Waco: Baylor University Press, 2005.

Lambert, Frank. *"Pedlar in Divinity": George Whitefield and the Transatlantic Revivals, 1737-1770.* Princeton: Princeton University Press, 1994.

Larsen, Timothy. "Defining and Locating Evangelicalism." In *The Cambridge Companion to Evangelical Theology,* edited by Timothy Larsen and Daniel J. Treier. Cambridge: Cambridge University Press, 2007.

Lathrop, Gordon. "Bath, Word, Prayer, Table: Reflections on Doing the Liturgical Ordo in a Postmodern Time." In *Ordo: Bath, Word, Prayer, Table: A Liturgical Primer in Honor of Gordon W. Lathrop,* edited by Dirk G. Lange and Dwight W. Vogel. Akron: OSL Publications, 2005.

————. *Central Things: Worship in Word and Sacrament.* Minneapolis: Augsburg Fortress Press, 2005.

————. *The Four Gospels on Sunday: The New Testament and the Reform of Christian Worship.* Minneapolis: Fortress Press, 2011.

————. *Holy Ground: A Liturgical Cosmology.* Minneapolis: Fortress Press, 2003.

————. *Holy People: A Liturgical Ecclesiology.* Minneapolis: Fortress Press, 1999.

————. *Holy Things: A Liturgical Theology.* Minneapolis: Fortress Press, 1993.

————. "New Pentecost or Joseph's Britches? Reflections on the History and Meaning of the Worship Ordo in the Megachurches." *Worship* 76, no. 6 (2001): 521-38.

————. "A Rebirth of Images: On the Use of the Bible in Liturgy." *Worship* 58, no. 4 (1984): 291-304.

————. "Worship in the Twenty-First Century: Ordo." *Currents in Theology and Mission* 26, no. 4 (1999): 283-91.

Leithart, Peter. "What's Wrong with Evangelical Theology?" *First Things* 65 (1996): 19-21.

Lindbeck, George A. *The Nature of Doctrine: Religion and Theology in a Postliberal Age.* London: SPCK, 1984.

————. "Two Kinds of Ecumenism: Unitive and Interdenominational." *Gregorianum* 70, no. 4 (1989): 647-60.

Losel, Steffen. "What Sacred Symbols Say about Strangers and Strawberries: Gordon W. Lathrop's Liturgical Theology in Review." *Journal of Religion* 85, no. 4 (2005): 634-48.

Mahaffey, Jerome Dean. *Preaching Politics: The Religious Rhetoric of George Whitefield and the Founding of a New Nation.* Waco: Baylor University Press, 2007.

Margin, Roger H. *Evangelicals United: Ecumenical Stirrings in Pre-Victorian Britain, 1795-1830.* London: Scarecrow Press, 1983.

Marshall, Howard. "Climbing Ropes, Ellipses, and Symphonies: The Relation between Biblical and Systematic Theology." In *A Pathway into the Holy Scripture,* edited by Philip E. Satterthwaite and David F. Wright, pp. 199-219. Grand Rapids: Wm. B. Eerdmans, 1994.

Marshall, Paul V. "Reconsidering 'Liturgical Theology': Is There a Lex Orandi for All Christians?" *Studia Liturgica* 25 (1995): 129-50.

Marty, Martin E. *The Christian World: A Global History.* New York: Modern Library, 2007.

———. *Righteous Empire: The Protestant Experience in America.* New York: Dial Press, 1970.

McGrath, Alister, and David Wenham. "Evangelicalism and Biblical Authority." In *Evangelical Anglicans: Their Role and Influence in the Church Today,* edited by R. T. France and A. E. McGrath. London: SPCK, 1993.

Menken, Martinus J. J. "John 6:51c-58: Eucharist or Christology?" In *Critical Readings of John 6,* edited by R. Alan Culpepper. Leiden: E. J. Brill, 1997.

Migliore, Daniel L. *Faith Seeking Understanding: An Introduction to Christian Theology.* Grand Rapids: Wm. B. Eerdmans, 1991.

Mitchell, Nathan. *Meeting Mystery: Liturgy, Worship, Sacraments.* Maryknoll, N.Y.: Orbis Books, 2006.

Morgenthaler, Sally. "An Emerging Worship Response." In *Exploring the Worship Spectrum,* edited by Paul F. Zahl and Harold Best. Grand Rapids: Zondervan, 2004.

———. "Worship as Evangelism: Sally Morgenthaler Rethinks Her Own Paradigm." *Rev! Magazine* (May/June 2007): 48-53.

———. *Worship Evangelism: Inviting Believers into the Presence of God.* Grand Rapids: Zondervan, 1995.

Mouw, Richard J. *Consulting the Faithful: What Christian Intellectuals Can Learn from Popular Religion.* Grand Rapids: Wm. B. Eerdmans, 1994.

———. "The Problem of Authority in Evangelical Christianity." In *Church Unity and the Papal Office,* edited by Carl E. Braaten and Robert W. Jenson, pp. 124-41. Grand Rapids: Wm. B. Eerdmans, 2001.

Murphy, Nancey. *Beyond Liberalism and Fundamentalism: How Modern and Post-Modern Philosophy Set the Theological Agenda.* London and New York: Continuum/Trinity Press International, 1996.

Noll, Mark A. *Between Faith and Criticism: Evangelicals, Scholarship, and the Bible in America.* San Francisco: Harper & Row, 1986.

———. "Comment on Robert Gundry." *Evangelical Studies Bulletin* 19, no. 1 (2002): 4.

O'Grady, John F. *According to John: The Witness of the Beloved Disciple.* New York: Paulist Press, 1999.

———. "Individualism and Johannine Ecclesiology." *Biblical Theology Bulletin* 5, no. 3 (1975): 227-61.

———. "Johannine Ecclesiology: A Critical Evaluation." *Biblical Theology Bulletin* 7, no. 1 (1977): 36-44.

Olson, Roger E. "Free Church Ecclesiology and Evangelical Spirituality: A Unique Compatibility." In *Evangelical Ecclesiology: Reality or Illusion?*, edited by John G. Stackhouse Jr. Grand Rapids: Baker Academic, 2003.

————. "Response: The Reality of Evangelicalism: A Response to Michael S. Horton." *Christian Scholar's Review* 31 (2001): 157-62.

————. *The Westminster Handbook to Evangelical Theology.* Louisville: Westminster John Knox Press, 2004.

Prokhovnik, Raia. *Rational Woman: A Feminist Critique of Dichotomy.* Manchester: Manchester University Press, 2002.

Ramshaw, Gail. "A Conversation with Julian of Norwich about Liturgical Language." *Worship* 85, no. 1 (2011): 2-15.

Riggs, John W. *Baptism in the Reformed Tradition: A Historical and Practical Theology.* Louisville: Westminster John Knox Press, 2002.

Robinson, John A. T., and J. F. Coakley. *The Priority of John.* London: SCM Press, 1985.

Rodgers, Margaret. "Scripture in Ecumenical Dialogue." In John Stott et al., *The Anglican Communion and Scripture Papers.* Carlisle: Regnum and EFAC, 1996.

Ruth, Lester. "Lex Agendi, Lex Orandi: Toward an Understanding of Seeker Services as a New Kind of Liturgy." *Worship* 70, no. 5 (1996): 386-405.

————. "Reconsidering the Emergence of the Second Great Awakening and Camp Meetings among Early Methodists." *Worship* 75, no. 4 (2001): 334-55.

————. "A Rose by Any Other Name: Attempts at Classifying North American Protestant Worship." In *The Conviction of Things Not Seen: Worship and Ministry in the 21st Century,* edited by Todd E. Johnson. Grand Rapids: Brazos, 2002.

Saliers, Don E. "Liturgy and Ethics: Some New Beginnings." In *Liturgy and the Moral Self: Humanity at Full Stretch before God,* edited by E. Byron Anderson and Bruce T. Morrill. Collegeville, Minn.: Liturgical Press, 1998.

————. *Worship as Theology: Foretaste of Glory Divine.* Nashville: Abingdon Press, 1994.

Schmemann, Alexander. *Introduction to Liturgical Theology.* Crestwood, N.Y.: St. Vladimir's Seminary Press, 1975.

————. "Theology and Liturgical Tradition." In *Worship in Scripture and Tradition,* edited by Massey Shepherd. Oxford: Oxford University Press, 1963.

Schreiter, Robert J. *Constructing Local Theologies.* Maryknoll, N.Y.: Orbis Books, 1986.

Schrotenboer, Paul, editor. "An Evangelical Response to *Baptism, Eucharist, and Ministry.*" *Evangelical Review of Theology* 13 (1989): 291-313.

Senn, Frank. "'Worship Alive': An Analysis and Critique of 'Alternative Worship.'" *Worship* 69, no. 3 (1995): 194-224.

Sider, Ronald. "Evangelicalism and the Mennonite Tradition." In *Evangelicalism and Anabaptism,* edited by C. Norman Kraus. Scottdale, Pa.: Herald Press, 1979.

Smalley, Stephen S. "The Johannine Community and the Letters of John." In *A Vi-*

sion for the Church: Studies in Early Christian Ecclesiology in Honour of J. P. M. Sweet, edited by Markus Bockmuehl and Michael B. Thompson. Edinburgh: T&T Clark, 1997.

Smedes, Lewis. "Evangelicalism — A Fantasy." *Reformed Journal* 30, no. 2 (1980): 2-3.

Smidt, Corwin E. *Pulpit and Politics: Clergy in American Politics at the Advent of the Millennium*. Waco: Baylor University Press, 2004.

Smith, D. Moody. *Johannine Christianity: Essays on Its Setting, Sources, and Theology*. Columbia: University of South Carolina Press, 1984.

———. *The Theology of the Gospel of John*. New York: Cambridge University Press, 1995.

Smith, James K. A. *The Devil Reads Derrida — and Other Essays on the University, the Church, Politics, and the Arts*. Grand Rapids: Wm. B. Eerdmans, 2009.

Smith, Ted A. *The New Measures: A Theological History of Democratic Practice*. Cambridge: Cambridge University Press, 2007.

Staton, John E. "A Vision of Unity — Christian Unity in the Fourth Gospel." *Evangelical Quarterly* 69 (1997): 291-305.

Stout, Harry. *The Divine Dramatist: George Whitefield and the Rise of Modern Evangelicalism*. Grand Rapids: Wm. B. Eerdmans, 1991.

———. *The New England Soul: Preaching and Religious Culture in Colonial New England*. New York: Oxford University Press, 1986.

Tannen, Deborah. *The Argument Culture: Stopping America's War of Words*. New York: Ballantine Books, 1998.

Thumma, Scott, and Dave Travis. *Beyond Megachurch Myths: What We Can Learn from America's Largest Churches*. San Francisco: Jossey-Bass, 2007.

Tillard, J.-M. R. *Church of Churches: The Ecclesiology of Communion*. Collegeville, Minn.: Liturgical Press, 1992.

Tonkiss, Fran. *Space, the City, and Social Theory: Social Relations and Urban Forms*. Cambridge: Polity Press, 2005.

Valantasis, Richard. *The Gospel of Thomas*. New York: Routledge, 1997.

Vanhoozer, Kevin. *The Drama of Doctrine: A Canonical-Linguistic Approach to Christian Theology*. Louisville: Westminster John Knox Press, 2005.

———. *First Theology: God, Scripture, and Hermeneutics*. Downers Grove, Ill.: InterVarsity Press, 2002.

———. "God's Mighty Speech-Acts: The Doctrine of Scripture Today." In *A Pathway into the Holy Scripture*, edited by Philip E. Satterthwaite and David F. Wright, pp. 143-81. Grand Rapids: Wm. B. Eerdmans, 1994.

———. *Is There a Meaning in This Text? The Bible, the Reader, and the Morality of Literary Knowledge*. Grand Rapids: Zondervan, 1998.

Vogel, Dwight W. *Primary Sources of Liturgical Theology: A Reader*. Collegeville, Minn.: Liturgical Press, 2000.

Volf, Miroslav. *After Our Likeness: The Church as the Image of the Trinity.* Grand
Rapids: Wm. B. Eerdmans, 1998.

———. "Against a Pretentious Church: A Rejoinder to Bell's Response." *Modern
Theology* 19 (2003): 281-85.

Ward, W. R. *Christianity under the Ancien Régime, 1648-1789.* Cambridge: Cambridge
University Press, 1999.

Webber, Robert E. *Common Roots: A Call to Evangelical Maturity.* Grand Rapids:
Zondervan, 1978.

———. "An Evangelical and Catholic Methodology." In *The Use of the Bible in Theology: Evangelical Options,* edited by Robert K. Johnston. Atlanta: John Knox
Press, 1985.

———. "The Impact of the Liturgical Movement on the Evangelical Church." *Reformed Liturgy and Music* 21, no. 2 (1987): 111-14.

Webster, John. "The Church as Theological Community." *Anglican Theological Review*
75 (1993): 102-15.

———. *Holy Scripture: A Dogmatic Sketch.* Cambridge: Cambridge University Press,
2003.

———. "Locality and Catholicity: Reflections on Theology and the Church." *Scottish
Journal of Theology* 45 (1992): 1-17.

———. "Reading Scripture Eschatologically (I)." In *Reading Texts, Seeking Wisdom:
Scripture and Theology,* edited by David F. Ford and Graham Stanton, pp. 245-56.
Grand Rapids: Wm. B. Eerdmans, 2003.

———. *Word and Church: Essays in Christian Dogmatics.* Edinburgh: T&T Clark,
2001.

Wellman, James K. *Evangelical versus Liberal: The Clash of Christian Cultures in the
Pacific Northwest.* New York: Oxford University Press, 2008.

White, James F. "Evangelism and Worship from New Lebanon to Nashville." In *Christian Worship in North America: A Retrospective, 1955-1995,* edited by James F.
White. Collegeville, Minn.: Liturgical Press, 1997.

———. "How Do We Know It Is Us?" In *Liturgy and the Moral Self: Humanity at
Full Stretch before God,* edited by E. Byron Anderson and Bruce T. Morrill. Collegeville, Minn.: Liturgical Press, 1998.

———. "The Missing Jewel of the Evangelical Church." In *Christian Worship in
North America: A Retrospective, 1955-1995,* edited by James F. White. Collegeville,
Minn.: Liturgical Press, 1997.

———. *Protestant Worship: Traditions in Transition.* Louisville: Westminster John
Knox Press, 1989.

Witherington, Ben. *John's Wisdom: A Commentary on the Fourth Gospel.* Louisville:
Westminster John Knox Press, 1995.

Witvliet, John D. "From 'DNA' to 'Cellular Structure': Charting Recent Evangelical

Scholarly Engagement with Corporate Worship Practices." In *The Serious Business of Worship: Essays in Honour of Bryan D. Spinks,* edited by Melanie C. Ross and Simon Jones. London: T&T Clark International, 2010.

―――. "Teaching Worship as a Christian Practice." In *For Life Abundant: Practical Theology, Theological Education, and Christian Ministry,* edited by Dorothy C. Bass and Craig Dykstra, pp. 117-48. Grand Rapids: Wm. B. Eerdmans, 2008.

Wolfe, Alan. *The Transformation of American Religion: How We Actually Live Our Faith.* New York: Free Press, 2004.

Wolterstorff, Nicholas. "The Unity behind the Canon." In *One Scripture or Many? Canon from Biblical, Theological, and Philosophical Perspectives,* edited by Christine Helmer and Christof Landmesser. New York: Oxford University Press, 2004.

World Council of Churches. *Baptism, Eucharist, and Ministry.* Faith and Order Paper 111. Geneva: WCC, 1982.

Wright, David F. "Scripture and Evangelical Diversity with Special Reference to the Baptismal Divide." In *A Pathway into the Holy Scripture,* edited by Philip E. Satterthwaite and David F. Wright, pp. 257-75. Grand Rapids: Wm. B. Eerdmans, 1994.

Wuthnow, Robert. *Restructuring American Religion: Society and Faith since World War II.* Princeton: Princeton University Press, 1988.

Permissions

The author and publisher gratefully acknowledge permission to reprint lyrics from the following songs:

"Spirit, Touch Your Church" by Kim Ballinger.
> Copyright © 1990 Integrity's Hosanna! Music (ASCAP) (adm. at CapitolCMG Publishing.com). All rights reserved. Used by permission.

"Purify Me" by Anne Herring.
> Copyright © 1988 Latter Rain Music (ASCAP) (adm. at CapitolCMGPublishing .com). All rights reserved. Used by permission.

"King of Grace" by Mark Altrogge.
> Copyright © 2000 Sovereign Grace Praise (BMI) (adm. at CapitolCMGPublish ing.com). All rights reserved. Used by permission.

"Revelation Song" by Jennie Lee Riddle.
> Copyright © 2004 Gateway Create Pub. (BMI) (adm. at CapitolCMGPublishing .com). All rights reserved. Used by permission.

"Your Name" by Andy Bromley.
> Copyright © 1998 Thankyou Music (PRS) (adm. worldwide at CapitolCMG Publishing.com excluding Europe which is adm. by Kingswaysongs). All rights reserved. Used by permission.

"Holy, Holy, Holy" by Gary Oliver.
> Copyright © 1991 by Word Music.

"Wonderful, Merciful Savior" by Dawn Rodgers and Eric Wyse.
> Copyright © 1989 by Word Music.